Create Awareness from Within

From our center we establish our relationships with our internal and external worlds. . . . Continue to explore—not driven with the need to answer a hundred questions more accurately and faster than anyone else, but with a curiosity of not knowing and the pleasure of first discoveries. The right answers are only right for you. Create your own test; and with patience, curiosity, openness, and awareness, come to an understanding of how you present, create, unfold, sense, function, and change.

Stan Wrobel, Ph.D.

About the Author

Stan Wrobel has studied the art of Aikido for twenty years and holds a rank of third-degree black belt. Currently he is in training for certification in the Feldenkrais Method of Somatic Education. His interests include the process of learning and the ways individuals organize to function and move.

After receiving his doctoral degree from the Massachusetts Institute of Technology, Wrobel worked as a research scientist and technical manager in the chemical and biomedical industries. Today, he is a consulting chemist.

To Write to the Author

If you wish to contact the author or would like more information about this book, please write to the author in care of Llewellyn Worldwide and we will forward your request. Both the author and publisher appreciate hearing from you and learning of your enjoyment of this book and how it has helped you. Llewellyn Worldwide cannot guarantee that every letter written to the author can be answered, but all will be forwarded. Please write to:

Stan Wrobel, Ph.D. ·
% Llewellyn Worldwide
P.O. Box 64383, Dept. 0-7387-0060-6
St. Paul, MN 55164-0383, U.S.A.

Please enclose a self-addressed stamped envelope for reply,
or $1.00 to cover costs. If outside U.S.A., enclose
international postal reply coupon.

Many of Llewellyn's authors have websites with additional information and resources. For more information, please visit our website at http://www.llewellyn.com.

AIKIDO
FOR SELF DISCOVERY

blueprint for an enlightened life

STAN WROBEL, Ph.D.

2001
Llewellyn Publications
St. Paul, Minnesota 55164-0383, U.S.A.

First Edition
First Printing, 2001

Book design and editing by Joanna Willis
Cover design by Kevin R. Brown

Library of Congress Cataloging-in-Publication Data
Wrobel, Stan, 1943–
   Aikido for self discovery: blueprint for an enlightened life /
Stan Wrobel.—1st ed.
     p. cm.
   Includes bibliographical references and index.
   ISBN 0-7387-0060-6
   1. Aikido—Philosophy. I. Title.

GV1114.35 .W76 2001
796.815'4—dc21
                                                              00-069635

Llewellyn Worldwide does not participate in, endorse, or have any authority or responsibility concerning private business transactions between our authors and the public.
   All mail addressed to the author is forwarded but the publisher cannot, unless specifically instructed by the author, give out an address or phone number.
   Any Internet references contained in this work are current at publication time, but the publisher cannot guarantee that a specific location will continue to be maintained. Please refer to the publisher's website for links to authors' websites and other sources.

Llewellyn Publications
A Division of Llewellyn Worldwide, Ltd.
P.O. Box 64383, Dept. 0-7387-0060-6
St. Paul, MN 55164-0383, U.S.A.
www.llewellyn.com

Printed in the United States of America

This book is dedicated to my family—
Mauri, Jessi, and Tara;
and to the memory and spirit of Molly.

contents

introduction

Bookshelves are filled with titles reflecting the development of an art form. We find books on the art of war, cooking, motorcycle repair, gardening, a martial art, and so on. The word *art* has been used to describe many different activities or processes, as well as objects with aesthetic qualities. An art addresses specific learned skills and the use of those skills to produce appealing creations. Yet art goes beyond the mere technical aspects of an activity; it beckons the use of intuitive responses and evokes a very personal expression that is loaded with insights, feelings, and emotions. It encompasses principles, processes, intuition, imagination, skills, self-expression, and the outcomes of specific activities. Its process possesses beauty and its outcome is beauty. It reflects our innate and learned skills, our originality or creativity, and a sense of harmony, control, and mastery. Art's reward is a sense of satisfaction in our abilities, in the mastery of the process, and in the expression of the truth of our being.

The study of an art is like a road map to somewhere, and each of us needs to determine where our personal somewhere is. For me, that somewhere is my own center, my own true self. Any art is a tool for self-discovery because of its reflective and expressive aspects, and this expressive aspect is most successful when it arises from a wholeness and truth that is unencumbered by personal history. With the actualization of a purer expression of self comes the exhilaration of personal power.

Art is not restricted to any one form of expression. There are many tools that can be used for self-exploration and expression. Aikido is one such tool. Aikido is a martial art that relies on harmonious movements and minimal muscular effort to resolve conflicts. It challenges our perceptions of strength and power and it challenges us to learn new ways of leveraging relationships to understand and resolve confrontations. Through the opportunities it presents to interact with others—both opponents and partners—it offers a reflective mirror to examine oneself. Aikido is a tool that creates situations by which we make use of something external to help us look inward to find ourselves. Our expression of what we find along the way will then become the reward of the effort and adventure.

If Aikido asks me to give up the concept of power through physical strength alone, I then need to look for new ways of acting in order to deal with interactions in a nonviolent way. In the learning process I begin to examine myself to more clearly understand the ways in which I act and the underpinnings that support those behaviors or habits. I begin to explore new ways to bring new power to my gestures and actions. I examine the many lessons for ways to bring those lessons out from the training hall into the everyday activities of living. The challenge we all face is to be aware of the learning opportunities, to be open to the learning experience, and to find the patience, perseverance, and wherewithal to allow change to occur.

Writing is also a process by which we come to understand different things. We delve into the facts and creations of the mind to find clarity. In writing this book, I searched for deeper meaning in the principles of the art of Aikido. I looked for insights with universal implications that went beyond technique. I also learned while I reflected upon my observations and experiences. And now I share these insights; not to seek endorsement, but simply to provide matter for reflection.

I also realize that in writing this book I engaged in a process, and just like the practice of an art, it is a continuing process to understand. Truth has its moment in time and understanding. On some topics I entered the process with some preconceived notions while on others I didn't know where the process would take me. In all areas, however, I opened myself to new expressions and to the mystery of unfolding thoughts and understanding. There was always a beginning, but the process by which I moved along the path was as rich with reward as reaching a milestone. There was flow, sometimes tortuous and sluggish and sometimes fluid and fast. And in those moments of rapid outpouring my writing was intuitive as if channeled from some inner source that I did not yet understand.

Perhaps the path to mastery begins with these insights. With courage and desire we test some now and maybe again at a later time. We see how they fit with our self-image, experiment with them, forget them for a while, and come back to test them in our reality of the present moment. It's all process as we sort through the stuff that our awareness brings forth for clarification and disposition. Mastery is the never-ending process by which we refine the self as we come to the center of our being from which all expression arises.

In the training hall we engage the unknown in the freestyle, multiattacker practice of *randori*. It is here among the uncertain permissibles that we demonstrate our abilities in self-defense, self-expression, and living in the flow. It is here where we demonstrate within the unimaginable the art of improvisational and intuitive living. It is toward this end that the topics of this book will be directed.

beginnings

|

Aikido is the way of harmony. For some, it is the martial art of blending the physical body with the force of an attack. Yet Aikido is the handshake by which we engage others in every interaction of our lives. It is the rapport we establish in our communications. It is the pacing we establish as we dance the tango, encircle another in a wrestling match, or move in a rhythmic embrace with our lover.

Aikido has its techniques. They are the means by which we learn to view ourselves in relation to others and to the environment. They are the means by which we try to preserve our integrity in relation to others and to the universe. They are the means by which we examine our own constitution—whether physical, biomechanical, intellectual, emotional, or spiritual. They are the two-way mirrors that allow us to see through to our opponent while at the same time allowing us to observe our own behavior, intent, and attention in the interaction.

Aikido is about process. Preconceived notions of goals or outcomes of endeavors can detract from the act and the art of living. The outcome of an interaction with an opponent can be reconciliatory, supportive, or violent. It can raise the emotional energy of your being or it can provide you with a pervading sense of calm and peaceful resolution. Between the beginning and the end there is life—observations, experiences, and lessons. After the beginning there is a flow in which we experience life with all of its opportunities.

Aikido has its tests, whether formally given by the teaching committee, informally experienced during regular practice, or when we apply our learning outside the training hall. As we engage in the unscripted, multiple attack of randori, we can demonstrate our abilities to weave through multiple challenges as we preserve our image of self, project our emotional, spiritual, and physical maturity, live in moment after moment, and thus, experience the flow.

And as part of the flow of observing, sensing, learning, practicing, and experiencing, we seek to accrue the benefits of discovering personal attributes that are closer and closer to those represented by our true essence. In this sense, our practice of a martial art for self-defense is a way of harmonizing the physical, intellectual, emotional, and spiritual aspects within ourselves. With such harmonization, a peaceful union with others and with our environment becomes more probable. Our practice of such an art is a way of revealing to ourselves finer and clearer representations of who we truly are.

We are continually refining our self-images and the ways those images are expressed in the way we function or act. Cycles repeat themselves on an evolving spiral; and learning processes must begin again— each time with greater knowledge and wisdom available to support the process.

II

But what makes us want to continue or to begin again? Why do some individuals spend a significant portion of their lifetime committed to the study of something like Aikido while others try and give up? At one time I figured that about 5 percent of the individuals who enter the training school for the study of Aikido continue to practice for any significant number of years. And among that 5 percent there will be some who never stepped away while others would have come and gone and come back again. Of the latter group, what is it that takes them away and, more importantly, what is it that brings them back?

There certainly is a physical component to Aikido. Enrollments take a jump after the release of a new action movie in which the protagonist displays his or her skills in the art. Visions of replacing the lead's image with our own drive us to the nearest *dojo* to embark upon a training program that may provide us with a new sense of self and mastery on the streets. Whether or not we are consciously aware of it, perhaps it is this desire for a change in our self-image that entices us to try something new—especially something dramatic.

The early training days and years provide exercise, new skills in physical self-defense, and a sense of accomplishment as one progresses through a ranking system with each formal test. However, many will disappear early because their bodies aren't ready for the physical exertion, their minds and bodies aren't coordinated well enough to give them a sense of competitive performance with their peers, or simply because the anticipated appeal of the art was not realized in the actual experience of it.

For those who persist through four or five years of training to earn a black belt, a renewal of their motivation is needed to help them define the purpose behind their study in the upcoming years. For them there is a display of a basic understanding, but probably not a mastery, of the techniques that define the art. For them there is a new self-image that is frequently seen in the new way of movement once the black belt and skirt-like *hakama* have become part of their personal presentation. Perhaps it is just the benefit of the hakama that gives them an appearance of greater fluidity and mastery; but they accept the felt sense of accomplishment whether or not it truly represents their new level of performance.

An old saying says that the real training begins once the black belt has been earned. Everything that preceded that stage was prefatory. So we are ready to begin learning again, but what?

III

Learning is a process of gaining knowledge and assimilating this knowledge into a usable understanding. And learning leads to a mastery of skills. Within the art of Aikido there are, for example, the codified techniques that characterize the art, and within these techniques are implied lessons that go deeper and deeper. To be able to execute the techniques, we learn something about the way our body moves and we

explore new ways to make such movement more efficient and effective. We learn that enhanced effectiveness comes from an enhanced awareness of ourselves
within an environment, and of lines of force that are
coming from the opponent. We learn that our breath
supports movement, and gaining mastery of this
coordination becomes another level of learning. We
start to acquire an appreciation of subtle muscular,
structural, and neurological activities, and we learn
how to integrate these refinements into our techniques. We find the power of the large muscles of the
trunk and the control of the finer muscles of our
extremities. We arrive at our center, that area within
the lower abdominal region, from where we learn to
initiate all our movements.

These are just some of the different levels that we
must arrive at in our physical learning process. Mastery, however, doesn't come all at once. When skill
at one level becomes more automatic, we can then
focus our attention on some other aspect of our art
that will lead us to greater refinement and ease of
expression. Old knowledge supports further exploration and progression.

———

Progression implies a process, and process defines an
art. So can the process be accelerated? Initial skills,

dedication, practice, good instructors, and an open mind can all help. But there is only so much that can be poured into the bottle at any one time. You most likely can read this book quickly by skimming some sections and paying more attention to sections with which you connect. Depending on your reading skills, the amount of content that you comprehend as I intended it will vary from individual to individual. Other meanings, interpretations, or similes that my words trigger in your mind depend on your openness and awareness. You may need to return for another read for further reflection or to get the messages hidden between the lines.

An old adage says that when the student is ready, the teacher arrives. But the adage doesn't describe anything about the teacher. We may assume that our next level of instruction comes from a new instructor, but maybe it comes from a different way of looking at the technique. Or maybe with mindful living we'll find lessons and insights in unexpected places and ways.

———

It always amazed me. She either could see things that I could not see or she had an unquestionable trust in the order of things. She wasn't reckless but only acted as if each step was a new beginning. What happened next could not be determined until the beginning had happened. *Each moment and each step was not predetermined or premeditated. Each moment and each step determined her presence in the only things that existed then, and that was the moment to which she gave her attention. She couldn't relive it and certainly didn't have the time to stop to think about it now. It had no value. She also couldn't worry about twelve steps ahead because she was only able to focus on the uncertainty and the experience of the moment. There was no time for the future, a future that could not be predicted with the same certainty as experiencing the present.*

It was amazing and beautiful. It seemed like reckless abandon; yet it seemed like every step was well choreographed. There were no slips or miscalculations. It seemed like she had done this a hundred times before and was now doing it for the one hundredth and first time with her eyes closed. But I knew that this wasn't so. We hadn't been here before.

There was no time for her to plan a course of action. There was no time for her to pause and plan her next step. It was all happening in a smooth and spontaneous manner. It was happening in the present moment. It was as if you were jumping from lily pad to lily pad—unable to stop for a moment for fear that you will sink. However, for her it seemed that at each jump there was also a sensory assessment of the current situation and a spontaneous adjustment for the next moment.

I don't know how it is done. I don't believe that it is a reckless act. My sense is that there was a desire to enjoy the romp and to release to the care of the Fates. If disaster were to strike, it would be dealt with in that moment. If disaster were terminal, there would be no concerns after that.

Molly, my golden retriever, was my teacher at that moment during our walk through the woods. For Molly it was a joyous romp through the bushes, down the slopes, through the creek, and from rock to rock—an adventure that for me was the necessary exercising of the family dog.

———

Teachers can bring our attention to new knowledge. Teachers, however, don't embody this knowledge for us. Only we can do this.

It is easy to write about, read about, or talk about concepts such as centering, receiving, blending, living in the moment, and living in the flow. It takes personal effort to incorporate such knowledge and awareness into our techniques. But it takes a much greater effort to take this knowledge out of the context of the dojo or the written word and make it workable in all aspects of our lives.

In Aikido training, we may begin with some preconceived notions of what we want to get out of the endeavor or what we would like to see in the final product. For example, on a very narrow scale we may be focused on learning how to execute a list of techniques. Our focus may be purely on the outcome of each technique—perhaps seeing an opponent pinned or cast off in some way. When we focus on the end we lose sight of the process by which we get to the end. In the process by which we get from the beginning to the end there are observations to be made and lessons to be learned. There is a flow which can eventually become intuitive, and if we are successful, we may be able to find a similar flow in the way we experience our lives.

IV

Our practice in an art is a powerful metaphor for how we view the world and our experiences in it. This metaphor provides further reasons for continu-

ing in a lengthy or lifelong study of an art, such as
Aikido. Taking the lessons beyond the safety of the
training hall into the way we engage every moment
of our lives gives our personal development tremen-
dous potential.

We can see how our body is a vehicle for communication. It tells a lot about ourselves and how we
interact with others. We have the opportunity to ·
determine through our skills and techniques whether
we are revealing a self that is highly conditioned or
more free and closer to our true selves. As greater
awareness develops, we gain a view of how we use
ourselves in interactions with others. We sense better
the intent and projection of our opponent or partner,
which allows for a more effective dialogue.

To develop our awareness we need to learn to stay
present in the moment. It is here where we stay in balance, stay open to running interpretations and perspectives, and can choose among options for our
response to the ever-changing aspects of the interaction. We learn about the value of rapport and of the
nature of power. As we receive our opponent's offerings, we develop our abilities to blend with and ulti-
mately take control of forces and lead the interactions.

If we want to talk about goals, then a vision of
more creative self-expression can provide motivation
to continue practice in an art. Goals, however, imply

an end; for us, moving along this evolving spiral path toward greater personal development is the real goal. A realization of the power and joy of releasing from conditioned behaviors comes from practice. The true self may then be revealed. The insights gained from practice support a process of learning and development that result in a more improvised, intuitive response to the flow of experience.

∪

Cycles are part of nature and a part of our lives. Cycles also show up in our training. When we begin, we focus on learning a technique and on demonstrating our ability to control our practice opponent— even with just a crude understanding of the technique. If our partner is fully cooperative, then a false sense of mastery of the technique may be experienced. If the partner is somewhat resistant for whatever reason, we will question the effectiveness of the technique or experience frustration in our abilities. In any case, our focus is still primarily external toward the opponent we want to control.

We can execute big or small versions of a technique. Early on in our training, we may work in big movements. We may be full of energy, with plenty to spend on the more dramatic, bold, big, circular movements. We reach out significantly, thinking that the action occurs at our extremities, and that the world to be conquered is out there. The movements are full of youthful energy and bold expressiveness. The flow of the movement engages our fancy and we consider it necessary for the effectiveness of the technique.

At another stage in our training, we find that the same techniques can be executed in much smaller spheres. Bold display is not as important as efficiency. Energy contributions to the technique are minimized, space requirements are reduced, and our focus comes to our center from our extremities. The techniques are the same, but the way we express ourselves through the techniques is different.

We then begin to appreciate that a technique defines a crude framework for achieving control of the opponent. Within that framework, however, there are many personal ways of expressing ourselves.

Cycles expose us to variations and options. They rarely repeat in the exact same way, but they let us realize that there are variations or flexibility within a theme and that such variations provide richness in our technique. Cycles give us an opportunity to do things better the second time around; they let us build on the base of previous knowledge or skills to let us realize that there are different ways of experiencing the events of our lives.

———

There are times when we need to forget what we think we know. Mastery never reaches conclusion. Movement toward mastery ceases when vision is narrowed and complacency in repetition drains our movement of soul.

Like writer's block, practice in an art reaches plateaus of expression. But interludes bring new freshness and assimilation of substance. Each level brings new ideas, insights, and skills. Interludes erase the blocks and allow us to further develop our mastery in an art. Let the interludes lead you to scale new heights, just as the pianist pauses before climbing an arpeggio.

Upon beginning again, we put an end to old ways of seeing and thinking, but not due to a sense of failure. We put behind us the ways and attitudes of locale, teachers, and of the self we knew then, and allow behaviors that still have value to become part of our bones while shedding others to make room for new growth. The past is but the feeding ground for the present.

Fullness brings complacency, stagnation, or eternal, but limited, satisfaction. So fullness must be reexamined, just as we must periodically sift through the clutter of our attics to determine what's no longer of value. Sort by value toward growth rather than by attachments to the easy, the rigid, and the false senses of security and mastery.

By beginning again and again, we are no longer mesmerized by the magic of the art or deluded by our mastery of its techniques. The magic deceives our egos and plays upon our narrow-mindedness. We must find new ways of seeing, and begin again.

———

Our learning is a process by which we take from Elsewhere for the purpose of greater development of skill. As with all aspects of our personal development from childhood to maturity, Elsewhere is full of teachers and environments that influence our skills, techniques, ways of thinking and valuing, and styles of expression. Elsewhere is full of rigidity as a need for control reduces variables and individuality and demands conforming consistency. On the other hand, it's also easier for us to deal with and accept a singular given than a multitude of possibilities.

With time, I came to the realization that there is greater value in learning how to learn than in learning facts. Why do I say this? Within the art of Aikido, I can pick up any of several books or videos that illustrate the basic techniques of the art. I can go to a few classes, practice a few repetitions of some technique, and convince myself that I am one giant step closer to my next rank. I learn where to put my feet, how to use my arms, how to cast off or make my opponent slap in submission. I absorb the teachings of the instructor and feel that I have understood the teaching, that is, until I attend another class, taught by a different instructor, who emphasizes a different aspect of the technique or a different way of moving within the general framework of the technique. What should I believe? Who is the better teacher to follow? Where should I place my allegiance?

Art is a personal expression. It is not a cloning process. The learning process leads to originals and not to mass-produced reproductions of somebody else's expression.

The learning process of an art goes beyond the recitation of rote-learned facts. If two apples plus two apples equals four apples, and we all agree to that, then what does two apples and two oranges equal? I'm sure that you could come up with many correct answers, some of which will be different than the many correct answers of anyone else. Should I lead you to your answers or can you find your path by yourself?

Artful learning is a maturing process that goes well beyond outward appearances. Those appearances are the expressions of emotions, creativity, wisdom, skills, personal preferences, and so on. But we don't learn these expressions from group classes geared for the transmission of basic facts to a mixed group of students with different needs, interests, values, skills, and senses of security.

So, how do we learn to learn?

revelations

I

Take my hand—in a handshake. Go ahead, take it. In your imagination, reach out, touch, grasp, and engage in whatever way you want. Use your imagination with all your sensory channels open; don't just visualize the encounter. In those few moments of our physical encounter, what am I telling you about myself? What have you communicated about yourself in return? If you are having difficulty meeting me as an unknown, choose someone else with whom you've had or can have such a meeting.

Visualize the coming together and experience it. See the outward aspect of extending your hand to receive another hand in return. Sense

> *warmth, coolness, rigidity, flaccidity, aggres-*
> *siveness, timidity, interest, boredom, coopera-*
> *tion, or resistance. Feel the other person. How*
> *do the two of you meld?*

————

In our movements we communicate with others. Interact with a number of partners in a single training class and you will have read a number of autobiographies. The manner of our presentations and interactions will tell us something about each practice partner. This is not done through verbal dialogue but through the manner in which the body presents itself, moves, and interacts. Aikido consists of encounters, engagements, and interactions. It is communication through movement and through process.

————

> *Perhaps the hand that you were meeting did not*
> *meet you but shot through you. Where did you*
> *feel that? Or maybe the extended hand provided*
> *no opening for you to enter; its fingers provided*
> *the only way for you to connect. Or were the*
> *fingers curled and the hand rotated palm down?*
> *Was there a connection between the eyes, or did*
> *the reaching hand move disconnected from its*
> *source?*

————

Presenting a study of handshake styles and their relationship to personalities or psychological states is not my intent here. My purpose is only to raise your awareness to the way in which two individuals can come together through a handshake. Awareness of this interaction can make you sensitive to the way you project yourself in an interaction, as well as how the other party engages you.

The body and its supporting energy and spirit have much to say. There are times when you can reach to grab someone's arm and you end up having your thumb bent back. You find no give in your partner; there's rigidity clearly being expressed in how this individual deals with others. When someone struggles to control their opponent with no softness or give of their own, does this reflect their tendency to try to tightly control those around them?

You may encounter partners who go through the technique, but with their attention focused elsewhere. Where is their focus in everyday affairs?

Others approach their practice partner with such flaccidity that they present nothing of substance for their partner to work with in trying to execute a technique. Are they always lacking in energy? Do they engage life with little commitment? Do they suffer from a lack of self-esteem?

And what about the individual who attacks but withdraws upon contact without follow-through and commitment?

II

Imagine the experience of grabbing your partner's wrist. Reach with both of your hands for the wrist. Reach in a relaxed way with no aggression or overcommitment. Exhale as you touch, settle down into your personal energies, and feel for the language of your partner's arm. What are the first words you hear from your partner's body through the sensitivity of your touch? If you don't hear anything, soften. Defocus your eyes, take another breath, relax the verticality of your posture, and sink into the depths of your partner's offerings. Experience the present in slow motion to quell the anxiety of your emotional storms.

In the touch, embracing, and closing of your hands, what do you experience—in yourself and in your partner? Are the lines of force that you meet static, dynamic, forward, backward, up, or down? Are they powerful, weak, motivated, or complacent?

Read the intent of their source. Establish if it is to overpower you, to respond to you, or to casually move through you. Or determine for yourself what the first moment of exchange has to offer to you.

Stay soft, open, and listen. Feel for the intent, direction, and strength of those forces that you have engaged. In the smallest, imperceptible way take away the intent, or refocus the direction, or weaken those forces so that a dynamic balance prevents the execution of any technique on you. Experience the power of your listening, openness, equanimity, emotional balance, and controlled responsiveness in preventing an occurrence. Stay with the moment, and the next moment, and the next, always continuing this dialogue with your partner. Within the stillness, there is movement. Within the stalemate, there is control. Aggression is prevented; force is countered; harmony reigns. Experience the power of no technique!

———

When we practice technique with different individuals, we meet different challenges. Within the boundaries of form, there are shades of function. Differences in attackers demand subtle changes in technique—unless your strength is so great that it can overcome any force. But the way of harmony is not about physical power or strength but about blending with forces, whichever way they go, to reach a resolution. In practice, this means listening to the attacker's communication to allow you to make moment-to-moment modifications within your technique. Some of these nuances may be openly apparent to an observer but only your partner may perceive others. And sometimes your partner is surprised that you have been able to move with ease around the forces that were directed toward you. If only we could translate this ability to listen, sense, and modify our response to how we function outside of the training hall in every kind of human and environmental interaction!

———

We can learn from watching dialogues between neighboring partners. A strong grab with resistance is received as a personal attack. Perhaps it is not even intentional or in the awareness of *nage*. It may be, but can *uke* be sure? Maybe it's just easier to create a judgment and let that judgment establish the response. Uke counters, through technique, with strength deemed sufficient to break through the resistance of nage. A stalemate ensues, but uke is not satisfied with a stalemate nor is either one satisfied in releasing the blockage to allow further learning. Each now sees the other's strength as a challenge, and blindness to the purpose of the practice, together with the provocative introductions, prevent development of the interaction. It happens so often in support of our egos that we feel we have no other options. Who among the two will release them from this stranglehold on their creativity and openness to learning? Who will recognize that this is not the purpose of the practice? Which one will recognize that submission is not defeat but an opening to keep the dialogue going? Which one is secure within oneself to realize that the real challenges are bigger than this momentary infatuation with physical strength? And as they release to begin anew, what happens when they come together again? Is there greater cooperation toward the learning process or is the need to prove a personal superiority continuing to inflame a challenge from which neither can withdraw? Are their horns locked and their movement arrested as they struggle forever to hold onto some piece that they claim as their own— and, perhaps, doomed to a greater loss in their efforts to preserve so little?

Note the more senior student's genuine attempt to help another student recognize the tension in the latter's technique: "Stay soft. Loosen up. Listen to the feedback that I am giving you. And relax—I'm trying to help you. Aikido is not about muscle strength." Yet, in return, the latter student also receives the unexpected hardness of the former's technique. Where is the disconnect? What does it take to be able to assimilate rather than to simply regurgitate our lessons? Does the message have to entice and mesmerize us, entrap us unconsciously with its bait, stealthily subvert old ways of behavior, and slowly nurture the emergence of new patterns of action? Why is it so difficult to see the internal disconnect between what we preach and what we practice? Is it easier to see in others the behavior that we relish; and why can't we realize the emergence of this desire within ourselves?

Stop and watch the revelations of the ages as they unfold within the safety of a practice session. Loud words and physical threats are not on display, yet the movements of two interacting bodies have stories to tell about the two main characters and the forces that have shaped their lives.

———

Imagine that you are interacting with, or practicing with, a husky, solidly built, strong, and grounded individual. You know the individual, and this familiarity brings comfort, but it also brings alertness because of the unpredictability of his behavior. He could easily crush a few of your joints, and just as easily release you gently to the ground. But you don't know what to expect at any particular time, and you don't want to provide him with a reason to switch from a gentle giant to a bonecrusher. By being alert, listening, and being aware of his and your contributions to this interaction, you can be sensitive to the way in which you project yourself into this interaction; and you can be constantly in tune with the way in which your partner engages the same event.

So imagine, then, that you grasp one of his wrists. Got it? That's it, grasp it with both of your hands. Feel his confidence and his lackadaisical entrance. He feels that he is in control. His face floats upon the air of cockiness. He doesn't have to prepare for the engagement in any way because he knows, or he assumes he knows, that his superiority cannot be questioned. You feel all of this and you accept it. There is no reason to challenge it, only to understand it and to respond to it appropriately.

By the way, which wrist did you grab? Do you understand what led you to interact in the way you chose? Was it a habitual way in which you lead into any interaction? Was it the way you chose to lead the interaction based upon something you sensed or upon the way you were positioned in the environment? Was it purely a defensive response to a perceived attack? Was it for some other reason that you can clearly see and feel?

———

Our movements reveal our habits—the way we think, perceive, interact, and respond. There are opportunities to learn about our habitual behaviors on the practice mat. Changing partners periodically during a training session allows us to socialize without saying a word. Yet so much is said in the exchange of sensory inputs clothed in the outward appearances of attack, parry, and technique. No grab or strike is exactly the same as the previous one, even in repetitive practice. Attention can waver, intent might change, and the patterns of muscular activity that support the attack show variations within a general form. Can you sense those subtle differences that challenge your perceptions and beg for individualized responses and not mindless litanies? Are we oblivious to the shades of meaning that each attack brings?

Do you choose to stay fixed in your response rather than openly receive the energy of the attack in order to absorb and reshape the interplay? What keeps us so numb to our patterns of behavior? Or if not numb, then what externally or self-imposed constraints keep us echoing a familiar refrain?

And then there is the grab—not so much with intent to arrest or harm but to suppress your response. The challenge is introduced, and your ability to recognize a shift in communication allows you to keep the dialogue going. The innovative replaces the habitual.

Would your openness to a creative interchange be greater if the engagement was not viewed as a challenge, resistance, or a personal or physical attack? How would you respond if the content were void of meaning or substance? Would you know how to stay focused on your connections through the fog of confusing messages? If in our *kokyu dosa* practice I gave you no resistance through my arms, would you recognize the futility of dealing with a superficial engagement and proceed to the core of my offerings?

Why is it that we so often get hung up on engagements in which we arrest ourselves, all the while thinking that it is someone else that is immobilizing us? How often in our practice do we notice that by simply releasing our hold we find freedom to counter techniques or escape immobilizations? It isn't our opponent who makes us powerless but our own deceptions and graspings of the insubstantial or inconsequential.

An artful practitioner will capitalize upon our debil-
itating ways of dealing with life's occurrences and
entice us to defeat or immobilize ourselves.

*In your mind's eye see and feel each of your
wrists being grabbed simultaneously and indi-
vidually by the two hands of your opponent.
What are you looking at? Are your eyes fixed
upon your wrists or the face of your opponent?
Are you thinking about your uncertainties of
freeing yourself? Are you focused on someone
else as a potential participant in the attack upon
you? Do you sense what is happening to your
breathing? Can you free yourself to be open to
these inputs?*

*Now move your right hand toward and
under your left hand, bringing the back of your
hand up against the right wrist of your opponent. Simultaneously, free your left hand from
the grasp by pivoting your flattened hand about
an axis that goes through your wrist and move
that hand between the thumb and index finger
of your opponent's hand. Your left hand is now
free to do as it pleases while your opponent's
right hand is immobilized against her left
wrist. But how is she immobilized? Is she hand-*

*cuffed by the active involvement or is she fooled
into believing that she is locked up?*

———

Every action has an equal and opposite reaction. Self-
preservation is a powerful force. More often than not,
when we are being immobilized or thrown, we are
attentive to the messages of our opponent's technique
and movement. Anticipation of the result or conse-
quences makes us prepare for what we perceive is
inevitable. We sharpen our focus to the first sign of
pain or imminent injury to our fingers, wrists,
elbows, shoulders, or necks and we respond with protective resistance. When we are about to be thrown
down onto the mat, we tighten our muscles into a
protective armor, hoping to minimize the effects of
our bodies' impact on the ground. Or we wish that
the same muscular contractions would negate the
forces of gravity and technique and allow us to float
rather than crash to the ground. In anticipation of the
consequences, we no longer stay open to the dialogue
and we shut down in an act of self-preservation. And
as we succumb to the fear of the fall or the pain of the
locked joint, we deprive ourselves of the freedom to
respond with openness and relaxation to a mind-
influenced consequence. Natural movement reflexes

that are our bodies' primitive controls are ignored and protective reflexes bring about shattering conclusions. Does this not argue for the importance of *ukemi* practice in the preservation of oneself? How would the confidence of harmless escapes alter the way in which you meet life's challenges?

In practicing techniques allow your partner to be continuously comfortable with what you are doing. Say a threatening word and your partner will respond by counteracting your move (i.e., "My ego and I are strong enough to overcome your strength"), or by tensing up in a protective manner ("I am not comfortable with what you are doing, so I'm going to tense up to protect myself"). Learn to lead the dialogue with confidence, composure, relaxation, patience, and harmony. Let your movement speak in ways that maintains comfortable contact and leads the way to control of the interaction. Replace the strength of your words with the power of your technique. Provide nothing that your opponent can resist. Let your opponent find out too late that he or she has fallen under the spell of your technique.

————

Take the jo *in your hands and raise it above your head. Now swing it down, aiming it to land on the lower leg of your opponent. Picture your opponent using a similar weapon to protect himself from the strike.*

Perhaps you see the anticipation as he prepares to defend himself. Note the fierceness of his face, the expansive display of his chest, and the tensed muscles of his forearms and hands. He's ready to take everything you've got to offer in that strike and divert it in a thundering parry. You can feel his cockiness, his anger, his strength, or his reflexive uncontrolled protective movements. The target is clear and now you strike.

Now, pretend for the moment that you raise your staff to strike again. But this time you see something different in your opponent. His fierceness is replaced with serenity, his overstuffed display of cockiness with softness, his relaxed hands are comfortably cradling the staff. You no longer sense a swatting parry, but you anticipate a silent encounter that has no threat of reprisal. How does this changed perception of your target alter your strike?

If I no longer challenge you to strike me with your words, your actions, or your staff, will you alter your attack? If I present myself as nonaggressive, relaxed, comfortable within myself, resilient, and receptive, will you strike me with ferocity and determination? Or would you save this aggressive attack if I challenged you with might, highly tensed and defensive, and adversarial in my presentation of myself? Every action (our words, our movements, our personal presentations) has an equal and opposite reaction. Through our body we project ourselves and elicit responses by the messages we send.

———

The art of Aikido talks about the self and reveals motivations, relationships, values, spirit, and behaviors. But who will listen? Do you listen to the self? If so, yours or others? Will you listen to your attackers' revelations and engage in a dialogue? Or will you only see the message and forget about the messenger? Do you hear your attackers' voices not as a wavefront, but as a propagating wave, full of history and carrying with it conscious and unconscious tales to be told? Do you let your attackers' stories be told and support their actions and expressions until they are relieved of their burden or let the self be known? Do you battle their attacks or journey with them, attentive to their needs and desires, pacing your response to the ebb and flow of their energy and riding their wave, fully resolved, to the grounded shore?

Do first impressions count for you? How do they arise? Is it a gut response or an intellectualization?

What inputs did you welcome to allow you to make a reading—and, maybe, a judgment? Did you have pre-conceived pictures or videos of the ensuing encounter that biased your receptivity to the next tale to unfold? Was your anticipation of the next attack rewarded with an easy resolution or was it fooled by your own programming or groping in darkness which put you at a disadvantage, unable to respond in a controlled manner?

perceptions

I

Our movements proclaim who we are and how we want to interact with the external world. Yet the clarity of the message is tainted by the vision of the perceiver. Perceptions are conditioned responses just as movement patterns are. These perceptions impact how we view and interpret the external world's opportunities and confrontations, as well as how we see ourselves as part of this external world.

As a simple demonstration, imagine two students standing and talking within a narrow passage—let's say a passageway up some stairs or a hallway leading to an exit. You pass by them, deftly weaving around the obstruction that their presence presents. You make nothing of this and actually exchange some pleasant words with the two students. To you it is a nonevent. Yet after you pass one of the students turns to you to apologize for blocking the way. "No need to apologize," you reply, since you never even thought of it as an obstruction. It presented no problem for you and you had no reason to judge or view their presence as any kind of interference or confrontation.

Now imagine an attack in which a punch is heading for your midsection. The attack has speed, an intent to strike with force, and the potential for a powerful impact upon your body. A simple evasion by the rotation of the hips protects you from the potential harm of the punch and discharges the force of the attack. You can view what just occurred as an attack or as an uneventful interplay of another person's presence within your sphere of influence.

Imagine yourself traveling within the accelerated flow of traffic on a busy highway. Do you view others as inconsiderate, reckless drivers who have no regard for the rules of the road that you adhere to, or do you accept your movement as an acceptable challenge to stay within a natural flow?

And even within your internal world how do you sense your physical body in space and its parts in relationship to each other? This, too, is a conditioned response, growing from all the events in your life that molded the way you see the world. Over time these events etched your persona until the unbalanced and asymmetrical became the familiar.

Lie down on the floor and let the back meet with the feedback of the floor. Do you float upon the surface of the floor or do you impress upon it as if you were molding your shape into sand? Scan the contact that you make with the floor and note the differences between one side and the other. Establish positions of your extremities and compare their lengths and their orientations relative to your torso. Sense the symmetry, or perhaps, the asymmetry of your form. Then solicit the assistance of another to slightly reposition your body toward a more symmetrical arrangement. How does that feel? Do these small changes disrupt the comfort of the familiar enough to make them feel unacceptable—even though the form may truly be symmetrical?

How often do the words that come our way have no meaning to us? How often do those words fail to elicit the sought-for response because our use and understanding of those words are incongruous with the selection, assembly, intent, and usage of the sender?

Is disharmony a product of our perceptions?

Can you see the world differently? Yes. Is it easy? Probably not. What would it take for you to accept the new as the acceptable familiar, to replace those treasured ways of holding on to security?

II

Imagine yourself sitting or kneeling on the mat in the dojo. Overhead there is a fan, largely unnoticed because its effects are subtle from a distance. Look at it and notice the blur of the rotating blades. That is your expectation of how a working fan looks. That is how you relate to that external thing. But this one fan is not try-ing to create a wind-tunnel effect or disturb you by its insistent, active presence. It offers you another way of seeing it if you can only change the way in which you view it. Within the blur are four blades; find one, fix your eyes on it, and let it take your eyes for a ride. In the movement that normally hides the contribution of the parts, can you find the part? Can you change the blur into a slower movement by the way you perceive and by the way you interact with the fan?

Perception is an interaction. How much we want to commit to the interaction will determine the kind of information that we will receive. What we receive—input, plus interpretation—will determine how we respond.

If a strike comes, and I don't recognize it as a strike against me, I'm sure that I would respond differently than if I interpreted it as a personal attack. How would this understanding then affect the practice of your art?

III

If perceptions are conditioned behavior patterns, then changing the way in which we view the world provides us with a way of learning how to learn to do things differently. But why would we want to change the way we perceive?

> *Place yourself in a confrontation with your opponent who is challenging you with a series of unpredictable attacks. It is a freestyle one-on-one exercise in which you have to be prepared to respond to the unexpected. Experience the speed of the attacks and the quality of your response. In an instinctive response to protect yourself, your arms dart upward to ward off a strike to the side of your head. The momentum of the movement creates a crash between the attacking and protecting forearms. It's not a matter of controlled blending but of striking back in defense. Technique loses to your perception of amplified urgency. Another strike comes charging for your midsection. The closeness of the*

attack and its speed catch you unprepared. Your shoulders reach for the sky and draw your center in an unwanted ascension. Evasion is gained at the expense of controlled reception and technique. Your opponent whirls at you with a backhanded fist. Intent is hidden by your opponent's turned-away body and it gives no prefatory warning or prelude to any of your recognized forms of attack.

The attacks ease off to give you a chance to recoup and try again. This time you see the strike to the head and you respond appropriately with a shiho nage *technique. Another strike to the head and you anticipate well with an effective evasion. And yet another similar strike takes form. But alas, you alone completed the attack in your perception; in reality your opponent chose to change approaches. You get fooled by your own deception, as you perceive what is no longer given to you. The early form of the attack was only a feint, followed by a strike with a different trajectory. You defeated yourself!*

Bringing our own views and our own paradigms of the world to any interaction affects what we witness. That view affects how we engage and play out the interaction.

Change the speed of the encounter and what do you see? View the attack in slow motion. Just as it was possible to visually latch on to a single blade in a working fan, now change your perception of time. Let the moments of the attack unroll as single frames of a motion picture. Remember there is an active contributory component to perception. The kind of information that is received depends upon the involvement of the perceiver in the act of witnessing.

If our view is clouded by our own expectations, how prepared are we to enter any interaction openly? And what is it that we want to gain by receiving openly? It is truth; truth not in some absolute, objective, factual sense, but truth as the lived and experienced interaction between perceiver and perceived, an interaction that demands attention, commitment, and resolution in the context of the experience of the moment.

Discharge your commitment to be engaged in the perception and you get blindsided by a backhanded swing. An active presence awaits the many possibilities that may come from any direction. Preparation for the evolving truth of an encounter establishes a chance for a harmonic relationship that is fundamental to the development of the art.

Sensory inputs bombard us with alternative realities. It's like viewing a scene with many reflective and transparent surfaces. What you look at has layers of information relating to what's not only in front of you but also what's all around you. You choose what you see and what you react to. You choose your reality.

IV

Our biographies tell us and the world where we have been. They recount our experiences as we progressed from birth to adult life. They consist of stories created from facts remembered from our experiences—remembered as they actually happened or remembered with a dressing of wishful or conditioned thinking. But these tales talk about what we perceived as happening and not about what did happen.

You might ask, What is the value of such speculation? Contentment with what you have experienced is a wonderful blessing. On the other hand, the realization of lost opportunities that were never experienced could result in despair and grieving. Somewhere—at the extremes or in between these extremes—we stand holding our positions that proclaim our humanity.

Over the years, I have watched new students come onto the mat to experience what had attracted them to the art of Aikido. Motivations and priorities among students varied, but these practitioners all came look-ing for something to add to the substance of their lives. It may have been a desire for pure self-defense, the benefit of an appealing physical activity, the medi-tative aspects of flowing movement, or the search for something greater that is hard to put into words.

I've watched the movements of all these path seek-ers just as I have come to watch my own movements. Kinesthetic intelligence varied immensely over a cross-section of beginners. It was easy for anyone to see. Some moved with athletic prowess while others couldn't sort out left from right. Some embraced the physicality of the practice whereas others dipped their toes in the water and jumped back from the chilling experience. In a normal, natural, selective process some continued along their path toward greater proficiency while most of the others disap-peared. Their stories will only say that they didn't like the experience, it wasn't their cup of tea, it was too demanding on their bodies, or it was too hard to learn. In most cases we don't really know why they left because we hardly got to know them.

Their movements within themselves and in relation-ship to their environment raise the question, at least in my mind, of whether the potential for greater intelli-gence in the art lies within all of us. Are movements on the practice mat begging for greater expression from each individual? And if so, what do they aspire to? Is it to something in the philosophy of the originator that is genuinely attractive or just temporarily sexy or cool? If we grant that there is greater potential for expression within each of us, how do we recognize that potential and how do we know how it would be embodied if allowed to bloom?

Our movements are a reflection of all the environmental factors that have influenced who we are. We are the products of an acculturation process influenced by society, parents, schools, families, events, and anything that impinges upon our daily experience. The acculturation process shapes our responses. It shapes our responses that are either passing or entrenched as guiding principles for future expressions of the self.

If the potential for greater expression of movement lies within each of us, how different is the natural athlete from the practitioner who has difficulty sorting out left from right? Perhaps the differences in potential are not that great. Perhaps those differences are the results of perceptions and acculturation. After all, aren't learning methods heavily imposed by the preferred teaching method of the day, the school system, the family, or the dojo?

Movements go beyond the large expressions we see in the execution of a technique, the evasion of a strike, or the breakfall. Movements include the way we breathe, the way we develop structurally and functionally, the way we relate to our environment, and the way we sense and experience our own internal relationships. Movement is a product of and a shaper of our self-expression.

If you grant that within each of us there still lies unrealized selfness, shouldn't the practice of an art be geared toward discovering the true self rather than chiseling an apparent self in a rigid expression? Our art form, whether Aikido or something else, becomes the medium for self-discovery. It allows us to create from within ourselves and express that which is ourselves. Thus, the subject of our art is the self. Its path of study offers the opportunity to come to know the self and to refine the self, provided we stay open to the lessons along the way.

awareness

|

What I say in the form of instruction or suggestion makes so much sense to me. It works for me in a way that I think that I can clearly explain it. Yet, the message doesn't reach you to a depth of understanding that is reflected in the way you move.

Suggestions for the simplest movements aimed at loosening up the body at the beginning of a training class seem to fall upon deaf ears. "Let the arms swing freely as you rotate your torso left and right." "Loosen up and experience freedom in your shoulders." And still, what I see is the calcified movement of a poorly awakened body.

My words have been polished by my own awakening, experience, and practice, until they are fully treasured with a satisfying, embodied meaning. I think these words have the same meaning for you, but I learn that they are empty, not resonating with the same message that molds my movement.

Does the message need to be translated into something that you can identify with? Is my message too personal, does it lack universality? Or is it that you cannot experience what I say, and, therefore, the message is but a string of grammatically structured words that leave you still functionally deaf?

Are you not listening? Do you not understand what I am saying? Where is the disconnect between what I am saying and what you are doing?

——

Our movements depend upon our ability to sense spatial relationships and functional freedoms within ourselves and in the context of the environment with which we are interacting. Our movements rely also upon our perceptions of the ease and comfort of movement. This means that if you do not know how rigid you are within yourself, how can any instruction on softness and flow have any meaning for you? If you cannot sense how tense you are in your hip joints, how can you assimilate instruction on flexing and rotation in that area of the body? If your shoulder blades are frozen within the muscular bands of the torso and you cannot differentiate them from your torso, how can you follow instructions to relax your shoulders or let the scapulae give you more degrees of freedom for extension? If the familiar is comfortable, how can you explore something new if you cannot open yourself up to sense the new?

> *Imagine yourself involved in a kneeling kokyu dosa exercise at the end of some class. You are opposite your partner who is facing you in a similar position. She grabs both of your wrists and you begin your effort to unbalance her. You struggle to move her as you try different advances with your hands and arms to shift her balance. Your efforts, however, are unsuccessful.*

What are you aware of? What do you sense? What emotions arise to shield you from sensing or color your perception?

In the midst of the battle or in the midst of any communication, where is your focus? Does the perceived resistance freeze your attention on her strength or grasp or size or experience? In the process do you lose your ability to sense or feel?

Are you aware of your breathing? Are your shoulders stiff and raised? Do you move forward to unbalance your opponent with your upper torso only or do you involve your center into the extension? Can you feel any tension between your shoulders or in your neck? Can you sense relationships, such as your center of gravity relative to your opponent's? Is your center higher than your opponent's? If so, does that help or hinder you in your efforts to unbalance her? If you can sense this relationship, then you are aware of some constraints that are keeping you from acting as you wish. With this awareness you now have provided yourself the opportunity to learn to move through difficulties.

> *So imagine that you are locked in this struggle with your opponent. Your arms are rigid rods straining to lift and unbalance your opponent through her own set of hardened arms. Fixed in this position by your failed attempt to move her, you settle in to take in all aspects of the interaction. Your silenced breath awakens as you give it your attention. Your shoulders soften and relax,*

melting from the light that came with your refocused consciousness. You find a point in your opponent's torso that seems like the center around which she moves. It is too low for you to get under in your effort to unseat her. But as you sigh and soften with the release, you feel yourself settling into the mat and into a position from which you can rise to unbalance your foe.

II

Being aware is like listening, and it's not always easy to listen—just as it's not easy for many to move slowly or to do less. Attention goes elsewhere and tends to other concerns. But maybe it's the listening that is the distraction—just as too many facts can hinder an understanding. I can see the emotional charge of an altercation relegate self-sensing and awareness to obscurity. Frustration can overwhelm you as technique falls impotent to the bulk and stubbornness of your opponent. Or boredom from mindless repetitions of a technique can lull your attention into a sleepy state.

It's hard to listen when anxiety or fear fuels the emotions or when shallow technique or false strength prefers to speak. It's hard to listen when the "I" sees you as "it," an object of its subjectivity. And it's hard to listen when rigidity constrains the openness of genuine dialogue.

From our center we establish relationships with our internal and external worlds. In listening, our sensory antennae scan for information and bring it back to our center for processing and response. We reach out with our attention and intent in order to connect with that which is external to us. We establish a union rather than allowing or forcing a separation. If we never allow sensory inputs to reach us and become part of our experience, they get lost at the periphery of our extremities, or even beyond, and force us to depend purely on our sense of superiority to overpower or mindlessly control whatever we are interacting with.

———

Stop for a moment—listen. Where is your focus? What inputs are reaching you? Do you hear the drone of your computer, the buzz in your ear, raindrops dancing on windowpanes, you swallowing your saliva, sirens wailing in the distance, the grumbling of your stomach, the rustling of the overhead fan, the sound of your breathing?

Do you feel the heat of the fire or the flush of your skin, the wetness of the water, the fullness of your bladder, the texture of the bark, the touch of your clothes, the tautness of suspension cables, or the tension in your shoulders?

Can you taste the circus popcorn, the peppery enchilada, or the fiery reflux from your stomach?

Do you see the world out there or the fingers of your hand? Do you see the flowing river and the film upon your eyes? Do you see uke striking, contact approaching, a meeting moving to your center? Do you hear the silence of your blending and feel the direction of his force? Do you smell his lost commitment and taste your established control?

Do you see the buildings and the skyline and the ocean lapping on the wharves? Do you see the darkness lit with sparkles of streetlights, flashes of billboards and signs, and the glow of a full moon? Do you smell the sweetness of the blossoms and the fragrance of freshly mowed grass? Do you taste the salt in the air or the emissions from the cars? Do you hear the din of the city: its cars, buses, trolleys, whistles, horns, and catcalls? Do you hear the rush of the wind

*and the rustling of the trees? Do you feel the
calm and the silence that pervades and over-
shadows this whole scene? Do you feel your place
in the scene—reaching and receiving and participating and contributing? Do you sense your
openness to inputs from afar and from within?
Do you realize your place in the picture that you
are taking in?*

———

Our ability to sense and to feel makes an experience
come alive. Otherwise, we are numb to the moment
and stand isolated as one object among many. Within
our awareness a dialogue in the present moment
ensues—touching, feeling, hearing, smelling, tasting,
and intuitively sensing other aspects within the domain
of which we are a part. Within awareness, unexplored
worlds internal and external to the self are discovered.
Within awareness, communion is established with the
energies that shape our encounters.

Stop again in your struggle to unbalance your practice partner and listen to the forces that are determin-
ing your movement. Stop in the midst of the exhausting randori and come back to your center. Stop in the
midst of the buzzing, clanging, and banging of tools
and find your breath and sense the tensions in your

body. Stop at the lure of another libation and find the inner balance that questions the value of the bait.

External experiences seem to dominate. As soon as my eyes reach out to you, I lose sight of myself. Why is it that we allow ourselves to be drawn so easily away from our center? Even in the case of the perceived attack, what value is there in losing sight of one's center of equanimity?

There are different personas that may be assumed in any response. Who within you is the first to impetuously jump at the bait? Is it the warrior, anxious to prove superiority or to defend with pride? Or is it the fearful self, jumping with triggered responses at the slightest movement? Perhaps the emotions set off the alarm, sending attention and movement shooting out centrifugally. Or maybe it's that aspect of the self that needs to show itself outwardly or prove that it possesses competency? If we are free of these roles, we can see with greater clarity.

Movement and its supporting motivations demand energy and quickly drain the self of its available supply. When practicing, notice from within your center the interplay of your physical, emotional, and psychological aspects. Notice if they support your fluid action, hinder it, or deceive it into making inappropriate, wasteful responses. From your center note the personality traits

and emotional and mind states that distort and unbalance the self and complicate any encounter. Who is it
that donned these traits and for what purpose? It's not
necessary to know for now, but it is important to realize
that they can cause self-destruction or very inefficient
action in any encounter. Let your awareness shed light
on these motivations, as well as on their resulting man-
ifestation in your movement.

Stop again and again and listen to the muse who
plucks your strings. Listen to the quality of the sound,
the clarity of the tones, the simplicity of the melody,
and the support of the rhythm. Does the sound rise
purely in support of the self or does a cacophony
of themes confuse your expression and defuse your
effectiveness?

————

*Stop in the midst of your freestyle practice when
the breath is lost, the movement slowed, the muscles tensed, and the flow disrupted. Return to
your center. Let the external action be suspended,
allow yourself to reconnect with the rest of the
picture, and reach deep within the self. Settle the
breath and relax the structure. Release the brakes
to effective function or movement. Note the separation that has been created between the self and*

*other. Within this regained clarity and aware-
ness, replace yourself within your exercise, make
yourself part of the picture that develops from
your center and not away from it, and begin
again.*

————

It's easy for me to lose myself in the picture. There's
all that out there for me to deal with—to passively
observe or to actively manipulate. How does it happen for you? Can your awareness be out there and
within at the same time? To act out there do you have
to lose sight of yourself—the way you breathe, the
way you feel, the sense of presence that your being
adds to the lived experience?

Test your ability to maintain an awareness of self in
any activity. I mean a constant awareness and not a
periodic one. Avoid waiting for the bell to end
another round of activity before you stop to look
inward for your center. Stay with that focus for as
long as you move through the activity. How long can
you keep awareness of the self at its central core?

Don't be content with feeling your pains or sorting
through your thinking or planning your next move.
Listen to your presence. Go deep to your center and
in that stillness let life proceed.

III

What is the basis of separation—between nage and uke, between "I" and "You," between external and internal, between emotion and intellect, between core and periphery?

There are no defining boundaries that create separation. Nor does distance or empty spaces create the separation of which I am talking. Space fixes the physical positions, whether it's within the body or between the body and some external object. Those positions will be forever independent of each other unless connected in some fashion.

Attention and awareness make such a connection. Awareness establishes the dialogue with that other and makes it part of your world. Awareness focuses that other on your active consciousness. In the process, a communion is established and separation dissolves.

———

Focus on your breath. Don't change the process, just give it your attention. Perhaps, however, you will find that your attention will unintentionally change the breathing. It's like the Heisenberg uncertainty principle of physics which states that the act of measuring or observing will change the state of that which is being observed.

Your awareness of the breath brings a new relationship between it and the sensing you. And this new relationship affects the nature and quality of the breath, as well as the movement of the perceiving you. The only instruction was for you to notice and observe; nothing was said about actively involving yourself in the process. Awareness alone re-established the connection between you and your breath. Awareness dissolved the separation that existed.

IV

Awareness allows for connections. Whether pulling weeds or using Sticky Hands to control an interaction, awareness is the glue that binds "I" and "You."

Pulling weeds, those unwanted plants that grow in unwanted spaces, is never an appealing job to me. It's a judgmental process where I kneel in a superior position, ready to decide on the fate of some sturdy plants that have invaded the empty spaces of my planned world of flowers, vegetables, lawn, and shrubs. With anchored roots they hold on to their piece of the universe, just as someone tries mightily to yank them to break their holds. Pull inattentively and the tops break free, leaving the core of the plant still anchored in the ground. Separation comes easily, but only of the parts.

Create a more intimate dialogue and let your attention and feeling course down through your hands and fingers, on down through the plant and its root system. No longer two, the plant moves with you. Your attention glues the two together, shaping and guiding your pull until the plant, in its entirety, releases its hold upon the earth. It's no longer a mindless force that acts but an attentive presence that seeks union and bonded, common action.

Sticky Hands establish the same type of communication with your partner or opponent. There is not grasping or forcing. There is only the contact that binds your hand to the part of your opponent that reaches out to attack. Stay in touch and listen to the movement of the attack. Stay in touch and prevent your opponent from establishing a new attack in the midst of your parry. Closeness is protection. Listen through your extension for union. Pace your conversation to the lead of the attack—wait, listen, test, and control. Let your awareness, through its effect on your movement, negotiate a resolution to the engagement.

∪

The student stands relaxed with her extended right arm resting upon the shoulder of her partner. Her partner provides all the necessary support for the arm that rests only under the influence of gravity. There is no need to expend any energy in positioning or upholding the arm. It is relaxed and releases all its weight to the supporting shoulder.

The partner removes her support and allows the relaxed extended arm to fall; but perhaps it doesn't fall but floats suspended, searching for alignment with the horizon. Its floating position defies relaxation, for rather than collapsing downward it calls upon the muscles of the body to hold its place in horizontal space. Need anything else be said about the awareness of the state of tension of that arm?

It seems like such a simple thing to do. And yet the literal understanding does not agree with self-sensing, with the awareness of self that defines orientation, tensions, and communication within and external to oneself.

The student tests her awareness once again. She asks her shoulders whether they are tensed or comfortably resting in a released state. Her comfort with normalcy suggests that they are in a relaxed, resting state. Only the eyes of an observer can challenge that claim, for to the perceiver, the shoulders hold stiffly trying to cover the neck and reach for the ears. The starting points of the two judges are not congruent. And yet a third, through the sensing of touch, may interpret the starting line at yet another position.

Place your left hand upon your right shoulder. Let the many joints of your hand mold it to the shape of that shoulder and sense the orientation of the clavicle, the position of the joint, and the forward/backward orientation of the shoulder blade. Let the left hand soften and feel the shoulder's hardness or softness and explore its contours. Is that shoulder alive? Do you feel any pulse? Do you feel it moving in concert with the breath or does it lie frozen, unawakened by a shallow excursion of the breath into that corner of the body?

Revive that shoulder—not with a harsh wake-up call but with a gentle breath leading and extending into the dormant zone. With your left hand, feel the rising expansion of the muscles and the repositioning of the bones. Let the movement in your hand and the underlying structures coincide with the movement of your breath. Let your awareness tie together these various aspects of wakefulness in the shoulder. Enliven the function of the moving shoulder. Let the incoming breath carry it to heavenly heights, pause to feel the openness in the lungs and the shoulder spaces, and then let the outgoing breath release it like a feather floating freely, but with a sense of control. Breath and shoulder function together. And as the shoulder sinks with the breath, observe if it plunges to new depths, not coerced by the force of intention and muscle, but by the release from newfound freedoms.

And with the left hand still sensing the changing shape of the shoulder, let the right shoulder slide forward, encouraged by your inhalation. Does it move in isolation or does it take a larger piece of you along with the move- ment? Sense, perhaps, the concave curling of the rib cage as the shoulder moves forward. Does the spine join in with a gentle twist?

Now reach for the ear with the right shoul- der. Jumping up will disconnect your organized parts, so reach up instead and solicit the con- scious involvement of all other supporting struc- tures and actions within you. With this rescal- ing feel a greater openness within you fill with a refreshing, more expanded breath. This breath brings with it lightness, less tension, and greater freedom.

Continue to explore—not driven with the need to answer a hundred questions more accurately

*and faster than anyone else, but with a curiosity of
not knowing and the pleasure of first discoveries.
The right answers are only right for you. Create
your own test; and with patience, curiosity, openness, and awareness, come to an understanding of
how you present, create, unfold, sense, function,
and change.*

VI

It would be easy to say that greater awareness of self
is needed to improve upon one's technique. Awareness has its role in the process of learning and in the
execution of techniques. Early on in one's training it
is difficult to cultivate such awareness because of the
greater focus on techniques. Progress is determined
by the number of techniques learned, by performance
in tests, and by the demonstration to self and others
that skillful learning of the art has been achieved.
However, in your skillful evasion of a punch, are you
able to sense the stutter steps that launch you into
your evasive pivot? Do you notice your rocking back
and forth from front foot to back before you actually
spin about your vertical axis? Are you aware that your
center of gravity floated up and down as you moved
with sweeping gestures? Do you notice that you lead

with the shoulder and rotate it prior to any movement from the pelvis? Does the late-moving pelvis
awkwardly back away from the oh-so-close punch?
Do you notice yourself jumping into the technique as
you rely on sudden, reflexive quickness rather than
move from a base of balance and serenity?

Does technique interfere with your movement and
with your awareness? Does the joint immobilization
or throw so mesmerize you that you lose sight of the
process by which you enter an engagement and work
through to its resolution? Art is a process within
which relationships are established with awareness of
the self and other. A dialogue is established, and from
this wakeful engagement a creation arises. The art is
not the final It, a subdued opponent, a photographed
subject, or a healed life form.

> *Take a forward roll and tell me what you expe-*
> *rienced. Don't think about what you're about to*
> *do, just simply do it as you would normally do it.*
>
> *What did you notice within yourself as you*
> *reached down to meet the floor? Did your*
> *weight shift forward as you leaned forward to*
> *shape your form to blend with the floor? Did*
> *you notice your place in space? Were you close to*
> *a wall, a line of practitioners, the prior student*

still struggling to clear the floor? As the roll wheeled your body across the floor and your orientation in space changed, did you see yourself moving in space with a progressively changing perspective of up, down, and side directions? Did you hear the clash of your body not conforming to the demands of the floor or did the silence applaud your blending? Did you feel yourself rise to standing as a plant rising from the anchored support of the earth? And in the gesture of this expanding rise did you sense your balance and readiness to move with the hint of motivating forces?

Perhaps you did your roll and only remember stumbling to a standing position. The rest of those moments between beginning and end are lost, never noticed, and never to provide you an opportunity to learn. Process was sacrificed, not necessarily intentionally, to the concern for the action and for the end. So try again with an awareness that puts you in the moment, that presents you with options, and that opens up a new learning experience.

options and change

|

In this imagined moment, sense your shoulder taken by a hand that intrudes upon you from your rear. The setting shapes the encounter and your emotions and habits forge the only response you know. Your action fails to free you, and instead freezes you as you strain for release from this intrusion. Alarmed or perplexed, a paralysis of the breath follows the self-immobilization brought about not only by the intruding hand but by the constraints of a limited, failed, and changeless response. The single-minded, unbreakable reaction sets you in stone and leaves you helpless to the ensuing consequences of the encounter.

———

An instructor in movement education once said that it takes courage to do less and to move slowly with awareness. The more common approach is to treat movement as an exercise and to use all of one's will, intensity, and effort to create movement, gestures, and expression.

When someone moves with focused intensity, it is easier to see the programmed repetition that forces action in what may seem as the only possible way. If that limited form of expression fails to accomplish its goal, then the frustration of failure subdues any rising joys that spark creative expression.

In an art such as Aikido, repetitive practice of a technique or a movement develops the motor coordination, awakens the sensory channels, and creates opportunities for exploring variations around the theme of a technique. It also allows the awakened practitioner to explore how modifications in movement or gestures can simplify a process and make it more efficient and effective. In the execution of a technique, note where movement is impeded and search for other pathways that provide the lead and control that resolves the encounter.

To participate and develop in an art is to practice while developing the skills, understanding, and wisdom that qualifies the practitioner as a skilled and learned individual. The development of an art is not an exercise in brute force and willful determination. Such an exercise approach can restrict self-development and prevent achievement of higher levels of artisanship.

Awareness of the self and of the self in relationship to others removes one from the rutted paths of personal expression. New channels are explored for self-sensing, for observing the personal gestures that characterize our movement and habits, and for establishing new modes of interaction between the self and other.

II

In a developmental sense, our actions are largely chosen for us. A parent's influence on behavior shapes a child's self-image in relationship to others and to the environment. Schools, churches, neighborhoods, societies, and cultures continue to provide the controls that limit actions for the sake of the common good, for preferred values, or for the control of the masses. Conformity and right behavior suppress individualism, and behavioral options are limited to doing it the preferred way. In this developmental climate, a limited power of action is realized by accepting a single mode of operation. Freedom is relinquished unknowingly to the control of others and the influences of the environment. Limitations become so insidiously familiar that the opportunities for other behaviors or expressions cannot even be imagined.

If someone grabbed your wrist and you thought that your only course of action was to try to pull your arm free, what would you do if your response didn't work? If someone threw a punch at you while you had your back to a wall, what would you do if you couldn't jump back? If your hands were held behind your back, would you feel highly limited in the ways in which you could protect yourself?

Constraints limit our expression and power. Whether self-imposed or externally imposed, they limit our ability to learn, to think, to experience, and to act. And their presence is so woven into the fabric of our experience that their treachery goes largely unnoticed.

As a simple illustration, the use of a computer to record my thoughts is now an apparent constraint. It demands my compliance with the systems of its operation and it draws my attention from my thoughts to the movement of my fingers, to the visual display on the screen, to the prompts and error notices, and to my inability to cross out and redirect with arrows. All of this slows down the translation of thought to written word. In my inability to adapt readily to this constraint, the expression of my flowing thoughts is lost, time is

wasted in trying to recapture them, and frustration with
the process tires me.

————

By its nature, Aikido is not aggressive. Attacks are
used to help create responses that protect the self
while leading the encounter to a satisfactory resolution. The attacks, whether strikes or holds, are the
constraints that limit our freedom or challenge our
place. The practice of the art challenges our perceptions, critical thinking, and responses to constraints.

In the earliest training classes, students learn to
safely position themselves in different ways to evade
or to deal with an attack. In addition to standing still,
you can step back, step in, step around, step to the
side, pivot around, rotate the hips, or extend to limit
the encroachment. You then learn that you can
choose from a catalog of techniques the one that
seems appropriate for the situation. In applying a
technique you can work to the front or the blind side
of the attacker; and in finishing the technique, you
can pin down or cast the attacker away from you.
Finally, through your control position you may further choose to change to another technique for the
purpose of changing the end of the encounter or for
positioning yourself better against other attacks.

Options are unlimited and arise always from an ability to be aware and to be emotionally and physically open and responsive to opportunities. In addition to the options presented above, a practitioner can call upon, in the moment, further relationships within space, time, and environment. Techniques can be executed in an expansive or tightly contained mode. Gestures within any technique can find expression in horizontal, vertical, and diagonal planes. Counterstrikes or feints can help manipulate movement in an attacker to establish desired lead and control. The attacker can be drawn away from his or her center or forced to rise up on his or her toes.

Options continue to grow as the practitioner learns ways to interject the self into the encounter. Within one's response there's a license to use one's own body in different ways. Movements can be initiated in different parts of the body to deal more effectively and easily with the initial constraints of the encounter. Spatial relationships of body parts unfold as the self is repositioned in the new circumstance. Muscle groups are called upon in different sequences to minimize the effort of the response.

And with the skills developed through practice, the practitioner can eventually begin to change from one technique to another in the midst of the flow of an encounter.

III

In the practice of an art, constraints and controls lead to new ways of functioning. But change comes slowly as releases from old ways of action only tease us with a temporary modification or refinement—perhaps only to let us know that there are other options for functioning. History fades slowly and the familiar returns to the sacred haunts within ourselves.

As further development occurs, our world of singular modes of operation changes to one of either/ors. I can have this or I can have that. I can do it this way or I can do it that way. I can paint it blue, or maybe green. I can paint my usual sceneries, but now, maybe, I can explore painting abstract symbolic representations.

As development continues, awareness and exploration cause more new ways of functioning to surface. No longer are you stuck with the limitations of an either/or world; now power arises from the freedom gained from access to multiple options. The power of which I speak is the ability to act regardless of the circumstances that present themselves. This power of options brings a new ease and effectiveness to one's actions in any encounter. With a greater confidence in your ability to vary your responses, you are freer to act in a natural, flowing manner. The feeling of being

75

stuck vaporizes with the emerging realization that there is no longer only one right answer to any situation. The only wrong responses are those that don't allow you to protect yourself and don't allow you function in any situation.

With the realization that there are many different ways of functioning, judgmental analysis of actions begins to fade. There are no longer only right ways, or right and wrong ways; now, many ways appear as avenues for effectively engaging in a life circumstance. And just as in the practice of an art there are variations in techniques and in the ways you apply the techniques, there are also options in how an interaction will play out. Options continue to arise when you are immersed in the encounter, even though you have chosen an initial response. The continued use of awareness and dialogue allow for an ever-changing and ever-adapting participation in any event.

For the novice, strikes to the side of the head during freestyle practice are met with either paralysis of action or an ineffective reflex response. As techniques are learned, effectiveness is incorporated into responses. Yet, automatic responses still dominate as the body is programmed to respond to stimuli in particular ways—not necessarily based on one's wishes but on a determinism that forged itself on the still habituated, unawakened, and reflexive practitioner.

———

Change happens slowly.

Take a moment to sense your wrist being grasped by someone else. You can decide whether this is an intrusion of your space from which you want to free yourself or whether it is something that you can, for the moment, accept and live with. It's your decision how you respond to the occurrence. And you can change your perspective whenever you want.

If you choose to free yourself, then imagine the steps that you will take to accomplish this. How many different ways can you visualize dealing with the task? How many ways can you resolve the encounter without compromising yourself, without losing your balance and serenity? That is, can you move without calling upon violence, muscular strength, judgment, fear, anxiety, or old patterns of behavior?

We often talk about how difficult it is for people to change. We recognize certain behaviors or habits and we wonder why individuals do not change them, especially if they are counterproductive to their work, destructive to themselves, or threatening to relationships. If change is generally recognized as being so difficult, can we expect changes in patterns of movement to be any easier since the latter is only a reflection of the core?

Change need not be a quantum leap from one growth phase to another. The magnitude of the leap may seem so large that it douses any desire for development. But the current state of behavior provides a personal sense of stability, security, and familiarity that an individual needs to give up in order to progress along the path of greater growth, greater skill, greater expression, and greater realization and appreciation of the self. At the same time, to develop oneself further, the individual needs to accept the instability of the unfamiliar and unknown.

By being open to seeing, thinking, and experiencing differently and by being willing and patient enough to test new ways of acting, the unfamiliarity of new stages can be tested while the anchor to the familiar is still in place. As the comfort level grows with some of the tested options, the new ways of acting become integrated into an ever-changing and developmentally growing state of security that defines a new stage of self-understanding. Learning has become an almost invisible process because the requests that were made of the system were not challenging to one's personal sense of security.

———

But why change from a state that is familiar and comfortable for you? Why not do just what you know how to do very well? Is that sufficient for you? Do you expect that that familiar way of functioning will always serve you well under any circumstance? Are you complacent with your current abilities? Are you satisfied that you have come to the full realization of who you are? If not, is it important to you to realize your full being in this lifetime or do you see yourself having your hands full with what you know and have this day? Are the task and the energy requirements too high to maintain your status quo? Perhaps newer options can bring more ease and comfort for you as you function in this lifetime. Is it worth a little exploration—especially if you can make it enjoyable? Can you make an exploration in which the risk is low and can you commit to something when the benefits are only poorly defined?

———

Three Aikidoka *traveled by different paths prior to arriving at a training seminar. During the days of the seminar they came to know each other and shared stories and philosophies from their training years in Aikido. One day they found themselves in a heated discussion concerning* kokyu dosa, *a training exercise that develops the coordination of the breath with a technique to unbalance the opponent.*

One practitioner argued that Aikido is about beautiful violence. Power is developed through the breath and unleashed in a mighty display to control the opponent. A second practitioner, however, defended his view that kokyu ho evolves from the molding of one's own body to the forces of attack received from the opponent. With the breath, the second one argued, the body stays soft and is able to move around forces until an appropriate alignment of self and other results in the control of the other. The third practitioner still challenged the others with his beliefs about the exercise. It is the projection of ki, *he said, that protects my sphere and repels the forward advances of the opponent.*

The discussion waged on and on for many hours one night and each one found flaws in the positions of the other two. Finally, a resolution was reached in which each practitioner would demonstrate to the others the principles of his own execution of the technique. The other two would experience the quality of the technique and then they would perform the technique in the exact manner demonstrated. Thus, each practitioner was to experience at least two other ways of approaching his art.

As it turned out, in the course of this exchange other possible techniques also arose. But in the end, each practitioner still stayed attached to his own views. The training at the seminar continued to its conclusion, and the three Aikidoka parted and journeyed back to their homes, returning to the practice of the way as they each saw it. However, the seed of other options had been planted because they willingly opened themselves to other perspectives and were able to find potential value in them.

Attachments to the familiar are supported by personal histories; opportunities for growth arise from releasing oneself from these attachments to allow for further enrichment through the art of others.

IV

Change is a natural outcome of exploring, testing, and using new options. With more ways of dealing with issues there is less anxiety, fear, and perceived helplessness; and with this comes an expanding ability to maintain composure and calmness. Judgmental thinking dissipates as you realize and accept that there are different ways of perceiving an event and that you have multiple options for responding to that event. You are less paralyzed. You are less concerned with doing the right thing since being open in the encounter allows you to act in many different ways. Options allow you to function in ever-expanding ways and to continuously redefine your image of yourself.

Muscles have memories that are expressed through tensions, organization, and function. These memories thus function to define ourselves as unique individuals. They establish how we see, think, sense, feel, and act. They capture our images of ourselves—images that are important to how we see ourselves as individuals and as participants in life's dramas. These tensions and neuromuscular organizations are said to lead to the creation of one locus in each individual around which all activity is organized. It is the kinesthetic fingerprint of the individual. Notice in a training class someday how some individuals make prefatory but inefficient and useless moves before they fully engage in the flow of a technique. It's as if their bodies can start an activity in only one way, and that prelude precedes any efficient execution of a technique.

These memories are the habits of our behavior. In turn, they shape our self-image, which is the way we know ourselves as functioning individuals. We experience a comfort with this self-image, which tends to keep us functioning in ways that continually support it. As change is adopted at the kinesthetic level, for example, a new self-image associated with a new posture, organization, and way of movement takes form. It may be adopted with comfort or it may seem as if flashing neon lights draw attention to the unfamiliarity and discomfort surrounding it. Internally you will also experience new sensations associated with the new self-image. To adopt the change you hope that the feelings of the new self-image support the change but it may be just as likely that uncomfortable feelings may make you shy away from projecting yourself in new ways.

The point is that our images of ourselves and our behavioral habits (body, mind, and emotions) serve the purpose of providing us with a sense of the known and they define for us who we are. Internal tensions function by maintaining this image in all of its manifestations. Therefore, include your self-image in your practice of your art. Imagine it changing and sense the corresponding changes in the supporting elements such as your emotional and kinesthetic intelligence. Imagine it exploring new ways of movement and feel the ease and efficiency of the strange but tempting new gestures.

power and the nature of attack

|

Somewhere in time past, another dawn arose in her consciousness. Another lesson broke through the barrier of ignorance and blind unknowing. It wasn't a bold "Aha!" but more like the silent penetration of water into an unnoticed aspect of one's reality until at some moment the unnoticed became noticed. It became apparent that what was hidden from one's awareness was always there, but hidden by one's reflection.

It was another training session, another hour of time squeezed out of a day of normal activities to repeatedly practice a defensive technique against a strike to the belly—before moving on to another technique against the same attack. Technique after technique fashioned to deal with the force and direction of similar strokes consumed her attention, making her oblivious to anything but her effort to evade the strike and execute a technique that had been demonstrated by the instructor.

But that one day, a message within a message arose. She saw in her practice a cultivated ability to defend herself from certain attacks. On the practice mat and in her imagination she knew some options that were available for her to wrest control in an encounter. But that one day, she realized that power was hers to give and without her resistance a strike to her midsection is but a strike to her midsection. She recognized that by only presenting herself in the path of a strike could she expect to feel the power of her opponent. Removed from the path, she observes only movement devoid of any effect upon herself. Powerless, that movement fades without personal harm—waiting now for judgment, emotion, and intent to shape a response.

———

How do we establish the presence of the wind if it cannot be seen? It is devoid of presence other than by its action upon whatever it encounters. The swaying branches of the trees indicate its presence, and whether the branches are gently moving or are being broken establishes the power of that wind. We know the wind by its movement through spaces and over surfaces as it ekes out sounds of joy or of disaster. When we stand in its way, we feel its presence as a cooling breeze, a chilling blast, or a disheveling turbulence. Circumstances determine how we perceive its movement, whether it's something pleasurable, annoying, or threatening.

The wind encounters the woods, anxious to shake up the tranquility. It will temporarily reshape the pliant limbs and trunks, but it will prune those that are brittle, rigid, and resistant. Those that bend and adapt align themselves with the direction of the force, letting it go by without passing judgment and returning to normal stability and equilibrium when the force has passed.

———

And so, on that one day in time past, the concept of power was no longer one based purely on a fear that arose from a perceived disparity in physical strength or from a perceived threat to personal safety and sense of self. Force of strength represents a potential that is witnessed only by its effects on the self, others, or other objects. Remove that "other" and the "action" remains powerless; or, remain in the path of a strike and grant that action a measure of effectiveness. Without working or acting upon something, power doesn't exist. Power is an assessment ascribed by our own perceptions that have been shaped by our personal experiences.

In like manner, harmless words can be received as a challenge, insult, or genuine regard for the receiver. What is our role in recognizing an action as an attack and how does our reception give belligerency to the innocent? And without an object to act upon, the energy of our anger is but a potential. How do you describe something if it has nothing to act upon— neither within itself nor externally? Resistance provides great opportunity for the expression of anger and provides a reflection that brings substance and strength to the emotion. What happens to that emotional force when its object remains unresponsive to the challenge and refuses to give it substance by merely offering compliance, agreement, or disregard? And furthermore, who has the power—one who has a fire within, triggered to set upon a resistant object, or one who disarms with a lack of resistance?

The corollary to this is that power is something that is given. By unwittingly or consciously relinquishing our independence, we allow ourselves to be influenced by something external, or even internal. By providing resistance to a force we give the energy of movement a measure of its potential. By a vote of choice we give the power of representation to others. By attaching ourselves to fear we allow fear to control our actions.

II

In the body of your mind, take a stance with one foot more forward than the other and extend out the arm and hand on the same side as the forward leg. As you ready yourself for another encounter, your opponent charges toward you and aggressively swings his arm forward to grab the wrist of your extended arm. Hand and wrist meet as you pivot around the front foot, moving to your backside and aligning yourself along the side of and in the same direction as your attacker.

What did you notice in these first moments of the encounter? Where was your awareness—outward, inward, or both?

In the action of that moment, what did you hear? Perhaps nothing. If so, revisit the encounter and bring your attention only to the sounds of the meeting. This time you hear the rasping sounds of your bare feet as they twist and slide over the textured canvas, but nothing else. Once again relive the moment and place your hearing awareness elsewhere in the scene. Do you hear the slap of the attacking hand on your extended wrist? No longer below the threshold of your awareness, the contact has information useful to your learning process. What does that sound of contact indicate to you about the meeting of the two, of the receptivity or clash of the two, and of the power of the attack?

And what of the sensory input from the touch of that grab? Did it feel powerful or weak, attacking or restraining? Return again and again to that encounter and explore your contribution to the felt power of the attack. Can you accept the force as a gift for your dance of becoming or can you only experience it as a challenge to your self-image?

————

The described movement to align oneself with the direction of an attack (*tenkan*) is a basic step in self-protection. It is practiced endlessly on the training mat not so much as a movement unto itself but as a preliminary movement embedded within a technique.

Yet, by itself this simple motion is pregnant with meaningful lessons which together provide an experience in learning.

Sensory inputs bombard the self as attacker meets defender. Sounds, feelings, and visuals describe the encounter. Emotional content and spatial orientation, proprioception, initiation, and sequencing of muscular involvement further embellish the experience for the awakened practitioner. A dialogue of touch is established and the value of options gets a personal consideration.

What do the sounds and the felt touch mean in this encounter? Does the sound of the assault that slaps upon the wrist correlate directly with the force of the attack? Does that clash impact the perceived power of the aggressor? And does the way that we receive and blend with a force determine our contribution to the perceived power of the intrusion?

On the training mat, the practice now shifts to the process while accepting the absence of real danger. The clashing sounds of the attacking hand on the extended wrist become a measure of the power of the attack. The felt touch of the same hand, engulfing and squeezing the marrow of the wrist, gauges the strength of the offensive.

Two yardsticks—touch and sound—now scale the interaction and provide constant feedback to the learning process. What options do you have to quiet the sound so that it is but a faint echo of the initial encounter? How can you alter your part in the encounter to soften the touch of the grasp until it is but a stimulus to initiate your movement?

Like wind acting upon the trees, blend with the force until the sounds disappear and the clutching hand is merely going for a ride. Constantly monitor these inputs and gradually increase your awareness of others as all contribute to the learning process. The power of the experience increases as we submit ourselves to new ways of acting rather than blindly relying upon the clashes that old patterns of action create. The power in strength is limited and is an advantage only if a disparity is in our favor. Learning goes beyond repetitive practice but embraces increasing awareness, patience, willingness to explore, and a concern for the process.

III

In the learning of an art, much attention is given to the outward appearance of the practice. The countering technique and its conclusion occupy one's attention as accomplishment brings a taste of satisfaction. Yet, how do we measure the quality of the interaction? What yardsticks do we use to assess this attribute of our actions? Is quality only determined by the output of our actions and not by the input of our effort? How would our attention to such quality affect our concept of strength and power? And, in the final analysis, why would you care?

———

She rose to standing from a seated, cross-legged position to face a challenge to her backside. Instruction showed her how to move from standing to the seated position, and her study for the day was to determine how to move quickly from the seated posture to a standing defensive opportunity. Countering techniques for control were not presented as part of the learning experience—only the movement emerging from the floor was.

Her experience and physical development gave rise to early success and a pleasant sense of accomplishment. After she acquired a sense for the course of the movement, she began a repetitive practice in an effort to become comfortable with the new experience. Up and down, up and down for just a minute or two before perspiration dotted her head and face and concentration strained her efforts. What appeared at first to be a satisfying accomplishment soon turned into a tiring endeavor. Increasing strain called upon greater use of muscular strength while interrupting the easy flow of the breath. As she reached her standing position, her movement expressed the finality of accomplishment before any defensive technique could be launched.

So how do we measure the quality of her movement, and, perhaps more importantly, the quality of her engagement of the interaction?

After a pause to recover the breath and to rest the unexpectedly strained, abdominal muscles, the practice resumed. This time awareness was brought to the breath and its relationship to the movement. Interruptions in the body's exchange of air indicated inefficient movement, and when breath and movement were organized in mutual support, greater ease of movement was realized.

With another pause in the practice, her body-scan still indicated internal tensions arising from her muscular efforts. These tensions affected the ease, comfort, and efficiency of her actions, maintained anxiety for accomplishment, and limited her ability to make adjust-

ments to any unpredictable occurrences during the action.

Quality was not in the doing but in the experience of doing. Quality did not speak to the goal but to the process by which she acted. Quality addressed the psychophysical elements that rendered a balanced body and mind throughout the action. And quality produced an understanding of the experience of the power of connection and minimum effort.

Awareness to the use of self thus provided insights to effortless action. The body no longer stumbled to a standing position, but rose with an elegant gesture and an undemanding flow of movement that still retained a continuing power of action. The upward, spiraling, evasive, yet engaging motion demanded no guidance for a continuing technique. Its expression extended naturally into opportunities for further interaction. Technique became not a means to be determined but a spontaneous, intuitive, and inherent expression of movement. Awareness expanded from the local concern for movement and evasion of threat to a global awareness of the self in relation to another within an environment of other potential threats and opportunities. Movement, once strained and attention-absorbing but now organized and fluid, was no longer demanding but an intuitive and natural response to the stimulus of attack.

IV

Resistance and tensions anchor the sense of self in a secure way. But security does not automatically imply comfort. How often do we hold on to behaviors even though we admit our desire for change and for a release from haunting, disarming, and unpleasant ways? Preservation of the self as we know it can motivate us in some illogical fashion, and our tensions give power to driving forces that limit our self-expression, personal freedom, and comfort.

Practitioners line up to take their turns rolling forward, backward, and sideways in a practice essential to receiving a defensive strategy that's applied to them. From secure heights close to the floor they rehearse shaping their torsos to meet and conform to the ground as they roll in various directions. The exercise repeats from a kneeling position and again from a standing position. All the while, the students must learn how they can adapt to a hard situation. Sounds and feelings provide feedback as new ways of softening the self, without collapsing, are explored. The training exercise progresses to breakfalls in which the standing body curls forward, projects itself over in midair, and comes to a cushioned landing on its side.

Aikido is a defensive art, yet someone must attack and that someone must know how to safely receive a defensive maneuver. The practice of the rolls and breakfalls prepares the practitioner for this aspect of the training program. From working alone to executing the rolls and somersaults in one-on-one attack-and-defend practice, the student learns how to adapt and protect the self in any encounter. Protection in the practice of the art, however, does not consist of counterstrikes but in "rolling with the punches," just as the tree trunk and limbs conform to the force of the wind.

Rigidity and resistance give strength to the oncoming force. Internal tensions build in an effort to further protect the self against the throw or immobilization, but they only make the defensive maneuver more powerful. In these cases, our personal ways of self-preservation create the potential for more personal harm.

The challenged practitioner will now seek another way to ensure his or her safety. Anticipation of the outcome leads the practitioner to avoidance strategies to minimize the impact of the receiving techniques. No longer does the defensive maneuver cause an action to the attacker. Now the attacker throws him or herself, hoping to eliminate the power of the defensive technique. Although preserved, the attacker is no longer fully engaged in the encounter.

So where does the practice of an art lead? To be fully engaged in an experience, commitment must be present. Commitment to attack requires an adaptability to changing forces in order to preserve one's physical being and sense of self. By conforming to the lines and energy of attacks or countering moves, power changes in the perception of the recipient. Resistance and tensions that establish the power of an impact give way to a blending that melts a force.

———

How often do we give up the power to act with comfort, ease, and efficiency? Consider the breath. To breathe is such an innate, natural process fundamental to living. It is a primitive process requiring no learning upon birth. As life comes and goes, so does the breath. The exchange of gases that the breath brings to the body is so essential that the body will shut down some of its function when the breath is temporarily arrested.

The breath supports our ability to function and to move. Intentionally hold it in during movement or exercise and realize that without it our ability to function is drastically impaired. On the other hand, coordinate its movement with action and feel it reinforce the organized movement of the body.

Yet we lose this primitive habit so easily. Simple attention to slow processes within ourselves arrests that breath as if its presence is a distraction to our focused attention. At the other extreme, dealing with multiple attackers in a freestyle exercise dissolves the same breathing process until movement ceases; tired and arrested in our tracks, we hold on tenaciously to muscular effort while losing the power of the breathing process. What are those other habits that mean so much to us that we overpower the life-supporting habit of breathing? How did we acquire them, give them so much power, and at the same time relinquish so much of the power of our holistic selves?

We renounce our personal power when we adhere to the use of muscular strength to hold on, support, and protect aspects of our self-image. The power of perception, awareness, understanding, harmony, and fluid movement is abandoned for impatient learning, strength, instant gratification, and environmental conformance. In the haste to learn, we function inefficiently as our energy is wasted when the recruitment of unnecessary muscles act only to distort the efficient functioning of the self. Learning becomes an exercise dependent on speed and competition. Brute strength and determination marshal all available resources for the purpose at hand, regardless of energy requirements, usefulness, and efficiency. Our energies are funneled into inefficient ways of acting. Expectations of familial, social, cultural, and educational forces create an environment that forces learning and behavior to conform to standards. Satisfaction is the reward for attaining the goal while the blind process buries its damaging effects deep within our unconsciousness.

It takes courage to do less—and to accomplish more! Will this understanding help you gain greater power to act?

receiving
and blending

I

Where in the realm of the possible do we give up our ability to act with ease, comfort, and efficiency? The appeal of effortless action moves most individuals to images of powerful expression, but intellectualization may not provide enough understanding to bridge the gap between theory and practice. Yet we continue to be mesmerized by the soft aspect of the art and by the simple, fluid, and undemanding ability to express and act in ways that seem so foreign to our self-image. Awareness, dialogue, options, and perspective all work to change our relationships in the lived experience. Blending and receiving provide new portals to the way in which we engage that experience.

———

In the kneeling kokyu dosa exercise, your extended arms are grasped by your practice partner. She settles into the grasp and secures you into a challenge to unbalance her. You wait to feel her energy and its direction as you look for a path of action that will lead to your control of the interaction. Soon you marshal your energies to initiate movement. Your hands turn as if to scoop up an offering from the ground and the forearms follow with an inward rotation. Your elbows drop in counterbalance to the upward lift of the hands that now face the attack and reach to buoy up your opponent at contacts near her shoulder fronts. You extend with a slight rotation of your torso to her weaker side and continue through your twist and extension until the opponent lies submissive on her back.

You withdraw back to your original kneeling position and await a repeat of the grasp, but familiarity and expectations do not yield the same success. Her advance shackles you, arrests you, and robs you of your freedom to act. Such constraints arouse the emotions and physical strengths to a new challenge. What was different in this encounter that led to such suppression of your engaging energies? That immobilization of your power to act—how did it rob your famil-

iar, effective ways? And where can you look for
insights that will allow you to grow in your art
toward greater self-expression?

———

Settled in his position, the practitioner waits for the
attack. Though skilled in his techniques he measures
the opposing force before he immerses himself into
the experience. He lives in acceptance and waits,
planning and hoping to act when provoked. He
receives the attack as something separate and foreign
to himself in the course of his daily practice. Once
the act is established as an unwelcome intrusion, he
measures the situation and decides to initiate a
response. Two forces come together, begging for the
active involvement and creation of an experience that
will lead to a genuine effortless encounter.

Separation leads to disharmonies, yet we stand
removed from engaging encounters and establishing
relationships—until forced to interact when set back
on our heels. Admonitions to receive the attack at first
seem like instructions to raise the arms and hands to
provide a target for the attack. What value is there in
such generosity, in such a sacrifice? Yet, what does it
mean, this gentle persuasion to receive? And how do
we go about receiving and preparing ourselves to
accept in a continuous, fluid manner the offerings that

impinge our reality? And furthermore, how do we establish a mindset that allows us to accept the unavoidable in a nondisabling, actively engaging, non-judgmental way—to accept it as our reality rather than as an attack or imposition upon our being?

What is the basis of our separations—between you and me, between nage and uke, between inner and outer, between emotion and intellect, between core and periphery, and so on? Our actions and our world get compartmentalized, divided into different aspects, each unconscious of the other and lost to the whole-ness that vitalizes the self. Disjointed activities and perceptions that fragment the self, weakening it in its interplay with its unavoidable reality, displace inner and outer harmonies.

> *The attack comes. It's real and you cannot avoid it. How do you prepare yourself to receive it? Maybe you aren't even aware of your anticipative posture. At what point from the initial sensing of the encounter do you enter into the interaction? Maybe you consider it a separate event that only requires conscious attention when it is inserted into a string of events that summarize your expe-rience. And when the attack is dealt with, you set-*

tle into a new time slot and wait for another event, another attack that requires your reallocated attention.

The practice of the art of Aikido, the continuous flow of attack and defend without pauses to recoup, speaks to the need to be continuously engaged in one's experience. Although on the mat the continuous repetition seems like a tiring physical exercise, its benefits accrue as awareness is given to the manner in which we stay involved and in which we engage each experience. Exhaustion indicates strained efforts and suggests new learning experiences that address the manner in which we engage with our breathing, pacing, and composure.

Entering an encounter is the *irimi*, or entering move, of the art. Should not all of the art and of living be an irimi? Rather than waiting to be immobilized or stepping back or around to evade a strike, irimi engages the encounter by entering, stepping in, or projecting forward. Rather than being an isolated opening move, it closes the distance between two bodies as they move toward each other and embrace the experience. From this perspective, who is the attacker and who is the defender? Both move with an active flow dictated by the unified movement of two as one. Separation ceases to exist as the practitioner joins in the interplay, connecting to the energetic opportunities provided by the encounter.

As the recipient of the oncoming energies, and participating in the active process of receiving, reach out as if accepting a desirable offering. Make use of what is given to you. Meld with those energies to create a vortex of power from which new expressions arise. Give of yourself to the expression of those combined energies until a resolution to a peaceful, fully expressed and resolved state is reached.

At what point, then, do you want to engage the encounter? Do you want to shape the experience or do you want it to shape you?

II

Receiving and giving are the yin and yang of our engagements. They go hand-in-hand as we interplay with the energies that approach or surround us. Receiving is not waiting for something to happen to you, to befall you, or to act upon you. It is not the unappreciative receipt of a gift but an acceptance whose act provides the giver a genuinely thankful return on consideration and generosity. In the process of receiving we also give in return.

Receiving and giving occur simultaneously—not as two separate events but as two aspects of one action. In the practice of the art of Aikido, one receives while simultaneously engaging, entering, and projecting into the encounter. The energy of the attack motivates the practitioner into a movement that combines a welcoming acceptance with an engaging greeting. In the resulting harmonious movement of the two, the greeting supports the discharge of giving energies while the acceptance draws and directs those same offerings away from the provider. Attacker and defender move in a whirlwind of energies that ties the two into one and brings separation into union. And in a similar regard, the aggressor gives energies to move the defender while receiving a return on the investment that leads to his or her own control and to a resolution of the interaction. Receiving and giving of the defender establish a complementary relationship with the giving and receiving of the attacker. This alignment maximizes the efficiency of the movement of the two and searches for a peaceful end to the encounter.

But what do we give up, if anything, in this blending of energies? To receive and give demands a release from the separation that ego constructs in our relationships. Identity that looms as a fortified island yields to a seamless existence pliant with all aspects of reality; this existence understands and accepts the effortless engagements that life might bring.

Receiving and giving as a simple, simultaneous event further symbolize our ties to each other and illustrate the interaction as one of a unit about and within itself. The polarity of two created by the ego dissolves into a melding of two within a newly realized, symbiotic relationship. Such relationships are always present but are not necessarily manifested. A practitioner moves fluidly within a montage of relationships whose realities become manifest by and within one's awareness—and always practices to embrace each planned and unplanned event.

Receive and welcome the attack. Accept its place in your reality, judging neither its fairness nor morality but merely recognizing its existence. In so acting, resistance, which creates fear, anger, and tensions, stays removed from the encounter. Action becomes more effortless, no longer burdened by the weight of our grasping. Separation caused by the discrimination between "I" and "You" mutates into a union where the other is assimilated into the domain of your control. By giving of yourself to the interplay and accepting its energies, you take on the other and its offerings—to do with as you choose.

III

Discontinuous patterns of engaging and acting interrupt the flow of our experience. Staccato defines the pulse of our combined engagements. Within the practice of the art a rhythm develops and the melody moves in a smooth and connected legato manner. Flow develops with engaging and participatory commitments while blending establishes the connection that allows two to move as one. By blending with the other or the environment, a wholeness is developed. Harmony emerges when distinctions perish and when one supports the movement of the other. Resonating harmonies amplify the energetic commitments, demanding less effort for a resolution. Less effort allows greater flow and greater freedom. Greater freedom from the constraints of ego and separation supports an experience embedded in the available energies of the moment.

Blending creates the experience. It consists of transitions through space and time, establishing relationships, and transforming and shaping the encounter. It turns the encounter into a creative act whereby intrusion and assault are transformed into stimuli to action that result in the continuous flow of self-expression.

Characteristics of blending include reversible control and emotional neutrality. Reversibility characterizes this control of personal expression through the rapport between attack and parry, subject and substrate. Such reversibility demonstrates the skillful control of the interaction without reliance on momentum, excessive strength, or emotional energies. Emotional neutrality with regard to involvement minimizes the drain of personal energies that weaken not only the encounter but also the development of the self.

Too often we try too hard or do too much. There is little trust in riding the flow, in effortlessly staying in touch and on top of the situation. Without effort it seems like we're not participating, we're not doing, and we're without a self-image that we can relate to. Effort, tensions, and impatience characterize our being.

Without these tensions, who would we be? Without these tensions, how do we imagine ourselves acting? What words describe the trust that provides the foundation of our securities? Can you imagine yourself being other than as you are—acting differently, trusting differently? Receiving and blending ask for a commitment to a greater belief in the self that goes beyond the egocentric reality of the moment.

Blending draws upon the elements of timing, space, and position, and it develops within an awareness that generates a true dialogue between the self and other. It transitions between options, creatively shaping the encounter as sensory inputs condition the response. Blending requires a sense of direction or alignment in which movement is timed or paced to that of the attack. Defense is synchronized to the attack so that the attack neither overruns the defense nor the defense outpaces the attack. Spatial relationships support the dialogue and allow room for movement and technique. Linkage between attacker and defender forms when timing, spacing, and position bring the two into proximity for connection and continued merged progress. In the alignment of blending, minimal personal input into the combined energies of attacker and defender adds like a sympathetic frequency to produce a resonating, enhanced effect on the joined outcome of the encounter. Effortless action develops as the need to do and to work hard dissolves into a control that guides external movement from and about one's center.

IV

In the imagined experience, see the intrusion that reaches to immobilize your arm. You see it coming, you know it's coming, yet the clenching contact freezes your response. What keeps you from processing the information that leads to the capture of your freedom? Are you tired, unengaged, separate, or thinking too much?

You stiffen as your sensory inputs turn into surprises that make you stop and think. Internal tensions and contractions protect in a reflexive, primal way. You have relinquished your authority to control the encounter and remain oblivious to those actions that further isolate you from the other. Who or what is it that truly immobilizes you? Is it the attack or some other internal aspects of your own body and mind?

Try again and sense what happens or what you cause or let happen as the approach nears. Are you waiting until contact is made before you move to action? Do you anticipate too much, move ahead of the action, and remain disconnected from the incoming energies? Do you let the attack push you upward, uproot you from your base, and brace, harden, and freeze you—from wrist to elbow to shoulder and so on—not into strength but congealed weakness? Or can you now imagine the acceptance of the attack as an offering that stimulates you to act in a wakeful, engaging manner? Can you perceive it as a gift that allows you to creatively express yourself in one of the many continuous encounters that con-

stitute our living experience? And then, can you and I do the same when the practice is over and we leave the mats to encounter the other aspects of our lives?

———

What happens if you are caught unprepared for an encounter? Frozen in your tracks by the surprise meeting, can you release yourself from the immobilization, create new movement, and enter the encounter at a different place? Enter to actively participate rather than be manipulated. Enter to shape and to control rather than be forced to comply or remain helpless to the provocation.

Can you create new movement by counterstrike, or better, by releasing the tensions that both the attack and your own reactions freeze and arrest you? Sense the attacker grabbing your wrist, driving your stiffened arm up, and bringing your shoulder toward your ear until arm and torso unite in an immobile structure that locks limb and core and mind in a solidified monolith. Now release the shoulder from your own clutches as you roll it backwards and downwards, establishing a small but effortless movement that restores freedom to action. And

113

> *let that new movement explore its liberties as*
> *you proceed to interplay with the attack*
> *toward a final resolution.*

So often we allow outside influences the power to control us without realizing that those influences are but the provocations that stimulate us to control ourselves. Just as fear can be a stimulus to new insights, external forces can bring our awareness to our personal, internal struggles by which we isolate and immobilize ourselves by our own actions.

So who tends to the mind and gives it the power to isolate, suppress, and control? Blending is the intuitive response, free from the constraints of experiences defined only by words, that taps into a flow that needs no creation but only a joining. It asks only for a release from self-imposed immobilization and reflexive protective mechanisms. Blending provides the natural lead and control that grows from the surrender of oneself to the energies of the encounter. Blending changes the encounter from struggle to flow.

V

> *Bone meets bone, tenderizing the forearm, as a*
> *jarring block that is meant to pass for blending*

meets a strike to the head. A felt sense of dishar-
mony rings deeply in the bones of the attacking
practitioner while the defender, seemingly obliv-
ious to the clash, repeats in the same receiving
manner over and over again. Is it unawareness,
ego, or just an inability to discover new ways of
receiving that blocks the learning process? If the
latter, what stands in the way of trying some-
thing new?

When receiving and blending occur without clash, movement flows in support of attacker and defender, of subject and event. When pain and bruises fade from the practice, each participant engages the event without threats to the self. Attacker's intent is unaltered and his security unthreatened; unmet resistance no longer inflames the commitment. Defender aligns with the energy, comfortable in the safety that timing and space and blending ensure.

My bokken is raised with intent to strike at the
instructor's head. Body and mind are committed
to the action. Defender stands ready to protect the
self with her jo primed to assist. I step forward
and advance the bokken as its tip moves in a
curved path from apex to intended target.

Defender steps to the side as she extends her jo forward to greet the advancing edge. I never felt her staff touching my sword. I never heard wood meeting wood. I struck, hit nothing, and felt swept into a void created by her perfect receipt and blending. Her staff engaged my sword in the silence of alignment where body and staff entered and adjusted until she took control of the encounter. Her staff came upon my sword and supported its cascading path, while my body was swept forward by the harmonies. And as my body fell to the lead of her blending, her effortless actions spun me from my course. I met no object and stood awestruck by the happening. Her aligning and merging added a small increment of energy to what was supplied by my attack, and in that attunement to the encounter, her actions reinforced my intent and my energies while supporting the spirit that I brought. In my attack, I felt no challenge to my task. I rode the wave of my energies until they subsided—not crashing in a pounding conclusion but rippling under the support of an unperceived tide.

controlling
and leading

I

Are there new ways to open up to challenges? Receiving, yielding, and blending support the discovery of new ways of acting. Unmatched physical strength is of no value in the practice of the art. We come to know strength and resistance more by the controls that they impose on the self. Growth in the art brings releases from the inefficiency or paralysis of old habits as new ways of interjecting oneself into interplays with others emerge. In yielding there is winning, but winning is an inappropriate perspective. In yielding and blending emerges a leading as control moves from the attack to the response.

Leading grows not from the strength of physical stature but from the expressive qualities of harmonious movements. Control shifts from the attacking initiative to the subtle allowances in the response that let the energies of the attack return upon their source or fade in a harmless shedding. Circles, spheres, and spirals, with their continually changing arcs, devoid of discontinuities that mark resistance, define those paths. Patience, openness, and dialogue pace the encounter, soften the receipt, and strengthen the response. The lead that shifts to the defender dissipates the intent, emotions, and energy of the attack into a final reconciliation.

"How did that feel?" asked Sensei. "Okay," came the reply. Perhaps a correct answer, but one devoid of much value for the learning process. "Okay," he calmly and quietly echoed. He paused, and then again begged an answer with, "But how did it feel?" Again came the same answer, this time accompanied with a little annoyance. "What is he getting at?" she thought.

"Did you feel like you were in control, moving effortlessly through the technique? Did you meet any resistance through which you had to struggle? Did it feel like you were leading the

effort, patiently on top of the situation, and did it feel like you could change the course of events as you chose or as circumstances dictated? Did you feel rushed, stuck, or like you were back-pedalling? Did it feel like your mind and breath were riding a wave, carried by your body that adjusted continually to the push and pull, rise and fall, ebb and flow of the encounter?" He paused to let the questions sink in, and then continued: "How did it feel? And if you can't say, please try again, this time tuned in to the experience and not just to the outcome."

Why bother with this line of questioning? If blind technique subdues the attacker and the technique adheres to the expected form, isn't that enough to demonstrate mastery? After all, the art is being learned for self-defense and seeing the attacker pinned or cast away is an accomplished goal. But maybe it's also being cultivated for some greater purpose that goes beyond the practical aspects of protecting the body. If this is so for you as it is for me, then we need to continue to look beyond the outward appearances to the felt experience. And in those sensations we learn to find and experience those qualities of engaging that impact our perspectives, sense of self, and control of our adventures.

With all of the emphasis on receiving, blending, yielding, and openness, the art may seem to be devoid of substance and positive action. Yet the receptive elements support a greater purpose as they transform the engagement through its harmonious movement into a leading that establishes necessary control. The art of Aikido is based on the principle that conflicts can be resolved without fighting and without anyone being destroyed. In practice we transform harmonious movement into a control of the interaction. With that control we lead to a resolved conclusion without destroying anyone.

———

Is control the object of our training? If so, what is it that we are trying to control? Are we trying to dominate, establish authority, or hold in restraint? Or are we orchestrating, choreographing, or directing all roles in our experience? Is our focus outward only, or does control begin with the self? Do we want to compose or do we want to subdue? Do we want to guide or do we want to command, contain, and discipline? Can we open ourselves to full engagement or will we contract in a determined preservation of what we hold valuable, fearing the exposure and uncertainty beyond our command? In receiving and blending, we align with the

experience, establish our understanding of the occurrence, and begin to explore the scope and direction of
the encounter. We assume the lead and guide the flow
after establishing the opening round of negotiation.

———

Sensei inquired again. "How did it feel?"

*"Well, my technique felt pretty solid. I was
able to do what I wanted to do, and my movement seemed comfortable."*

*"But you seemed rushed," he replied. He looked
at the attacking partner and asked the same question of him. "How did it feel for you?"*

*"I felt like I was being slapped around like a
wet towel. I felt the power of her technique but
it seemed like the flow of my movements was
always being interrupted. I was getting jerked
around under a tight leash."*

"And how did that make you feel?"

*"Well, I felt like I was getting penalized or
punished. I lost my control of the attack and my
balance, and I was getting buffeted around. I
wasn't being given any chance to reconsider or
to let my movements subside. I felt like I had no
control or say in what was happening; maybe I
felt like a ball in a pinball machine."*

Sensei directed his attention again to the defender. "Can you understand what your partner is telling you about your technique; and if so, how would you modify the way you engage the encounter in order to resolve it without arousing the same feelings in your partner?"

The two Aikidoka returned to the practice. The defender explored ways of establishing a different felt sense while repeating the same technique over and over. After a while Sensei began another round of the same questioning. "How did it feel?"

"At first I tried to pay attention to the smoothness of the movement—were we flowing all of the time or did we experience stop and go, with more abrupt changes in direction? I then tried to shift my attention to the transitions in the total movement—more specifically, to the timing or pacing of what I wanted to do compared to what my partner was ready to do. For example, after I took him down I tried to continue to lead him up in a continuing arc so that he had the room and time to reposition himself in a way that I would allow. I tried to be more patient in guiding his movement rather than forcing him to make sudden shifts in response to my anxiousness to move quickly through the technique.

"For a while after that it felt like I was losing contact with my partner. It seemed like the distance between the two of us was increasing; he was getting away, being thrown out away from me, away from my control. I guess I need to practice some more to find a way to control the encounter, stay connected, allow my partner a sense of safety, and guide the course of event."

"And then you will try the same with yet another partner," added Sensei. "Please continue while you stay open to the felt experience."

———

Within the "what" of the technique resides the "how." Within the course of events, we choose how we engage them. This is our power.

II

To control through domination, even if from a sense of responsibility, contracts the self while burdening it with restraints from tranquility and freedom. But by relaxing into one's being and into the experience, the practitioner senses the power to move in and within any experience in a safe way, preserving whatever is valued within the image of oneself. New realizations that emanate from the awareness of the self within the experience of the practice provide insights into the cultivation of self. Relationships change as the control of authority and strength shifts to a leading tempered by the wisdom of harmonious movement. Speed transforms from a measured unit to a time distortion established within the experience as we glide within and between events. We rely on awareness, space, timing, and immersion in the experience to preserve the self and other throughout the encounter.

Control grows from our fears. It is fostered by a self-image that's built upon the distinctions between good and bad. It provides a sense of importance, value, and power that supports a conditionally established self-esteem. Change the view of relationships, of good and bad, of right and wrong, of needs and desires, and control sheds its anxiety, righteousness, and authority. Control transforms from a domination of self, others, and nature to a harmonious coexistence where life is experienced in the natural flow of events.

———

The seduction of the oncoming strike entices a frictionless entry, free of anxiety or hesitation. Movement glides forward, grounded in earthly parallels. Arms rise to connect with the offering as the realignment of spatial relationships pro-

vides for the merging of two spirits. The touch captures the energy of the strike, leading it away along a path that spirals to the ground. And in the moving pause that stages the ebb and flow, the subdued strike rises to regain wholeness, supported by the generosity of a shared, coexisting energy. Resonance swells the movement before separation discharges the relationship.

III

Leading provides the passages that take us through the mysteries of harmonious movement. Uncertainties challenge us to stay open to the interplay of self and other. Movement is driven not by the fear of the unknown but by the creation of gesture in response to moment-by-moment offerings.

Leading changes the dynamics of the encounter. Attacker and defender become, respectively, follower and guide. The power to act resides with the lead for as long the lead captures the mind, body, and energies of the other. "No hand" techniques develop from gestures that establish the lead before contact is made. The gesture captures the attention, leads the mind, and redirects the focus. Reversals to techniques evolve as the lead is recaptured by shifts in position, extension, and timing. In a continuing exercise, two practitioners exchange roles as each stays present to the opportunities that the dance presents.

Leading preserves the security of the opponent throughout the interaction. Strong messages that challenge this safety suggest or demand reconsideration that spurs renewed aggression or resistance. Continuity in the movement leaves no gaps or lapses in the flow that offers new opportunities for countering. Excessive force necessitates actions to preserve the self and engenders resistance and intensity.

Leading maintains the wholeness and integrity of the self and other. Through blending and leading the practitioner retains identity, integrity, and induces the other to conform. Where superior strength or authority once established relationships, now receiving and giving within a nonjudgmental framework provide movement and flow.

The path of practice takes us over easy and difficult terrain. Deception lays its traps to ensnare or deceive egos that swell with a sense of mastery. Leading partners who through practice know how to follow make the practice of the art seem like wizardry.

Practice partners who are beginners provide reality checks. Their commitment to the attack may be tentative and their body movements encrusted and protective. Unskilled in ukemi, their concern for being thrown or immobilized colors their immersion into the attack. Their movement has yet to be conditioned. They do not follow unless it makes sense to them. How often do we follow even if it doesn't make sense to us?

Beginners may not understand that the ordinary practice of the art demands some structure to assist in the learning experience. Their attacks may be randomly shaped and ill conformed to the rigorous demands of some instructors. Resistance is still part of their action since they demand the proof that the art has some value. Beginners still don't know what they are supposed to do in order to function like the others. Unfortunately, "supposed-to-dos" still establish our organizations, schools, and families.

In your imagination, the novice stands ready to strike at your core. Unknowns fill your expectations of her offering. Will she give an honest attack, committing her energies to her target? Or will she strike in a tentative way with a feeble resemblance to an attack? Will she strike and stand firm or will she forge forward, determined to discharge her intent? Will she follow my lead or will she wait securely at pauses in the encounter?

And in those anticipatory moments you also question your actions. Will I be able to prove to myself and to the novice that my practice can truly display the way of the art? Can I receive and lead regardless of what is offered? Can I resist the use of force to make her comply with the object of the exercise?

Anticipating the worst scenario, you summon up your highest sense of awareness, listening, and leading. The strike comes and you pivot to avoid it. Aligned now side by side, your left hand settles upon the wrist of her striking right arm. You don't allow time for consideration as you coax her arm out to points that weaken her balance. The urging extends her forward, wrist connected to her core. The slack is taken up to ensure that connection. Her safety is assured by your guiding care to lead and to preserve. You feel her extension and her weakened balance. No time to let up; keep drawing her out. And as your extension reaches its limit, you change the trajectory. You launch her on a horizontal curve that takes her in a clockwise direction. Your extension keeps her reaching out beyond her balance. And as the tracking circle of her movement reaches the returning arc, you withdraw your left foot to prepare a welcoming space for her arrival. You open up now to the visit, left arm continuing to lead while the right accepts

and cradles her head under the chin. From your
tangential contact you now shape the outcome.

Mastery in the art of Aikido must be imbued with the ability to lead, but not with the threat and force of punishment. Alignment, exploration, and guidance must take the most recalcitrant or antagonistic along paths that preserve their senses of self, dissipate unproductive energies, and restore balance to a shared existence.

———

If some are to lead, then others have to follow. Through the practice of ukemi with its rolls, break-falls, midair adjustments, and releases, practitioners learn how to protect themselves from the conse-quences of aggression and resistance. Out of formed lines, students emerge rolling forward, backward, sideways, and over the top—from safe distances close to the ground to kneeling and standing and moving situations. Ukemi is the protection that allows for adjustments in relationships and encounters. It gives time for reconsideration of our actions without threatening our wholeness. It develops flexibility to adjust body, position, and alignment in response to actions encountered in the engagement.

Following the lead is yet another aspect of the art of Aikido as both attacker and defender develop skills in awareness and communication. Both participate in the learning process as the elements of the art address interactions regardless of the circumstances of engagement. What is at first the resolution of aggression becomes an interplay where body, mind, and movements blend in a passing encounter along life's path.

Our language has the power to uplift, confuse, condition, subdue, and destroy. Actions, circumstances, and values are described by words that fixate our thinking. Dualities of good and bad, right and wrong, attacker and defender, teacher and student, cause and effect, and follow and lead establish either/or frameworks that color our thinking and actions. For there to be a leader, there has to be a follower. There has to be, or else the concepts contained within those words of "leader" and "follower" cease to exist. But do away with the words, and what becomes of the art?

The art of Aikido is an interplay where I engage you and you engage me. It goes beyond the paradigm of attacker and defender. It cultivates unions where life just is and we create our experience. All of the descriptive words that establish distinctions lose their power to control our thinking and actions. In the interplays of our experience, we stay connected, spirits and energies merging in our reality. We choose our experience; but who are the "we" that organize the minds that shape our behaviors?

IV

Withdrawal and contraction are our protection. In controlling with domination we draw in that which we want to control. In so doing, we restrict our own openness and freedom while trying to subjugate the other to our wishes or needs. Our techniques reflect these tendencies. The tightness with which we hold on, the extension by which we relate, and the pacing by which we stay present and united address this controlling aspect of our actions. Pacing movement and response to that of the other maintains connections. Excessive force while leading either disengages the self and other or confines the interaction. Extension projects the self into the encounter with the confidence and safety of a marionette puppeteer.

Take the jo in your hands and stand ready to strike. Project your image of the self out to include the extension through the staff. Your personal domain expands as the expanded edge of your sphere defines new boundaries and relationships. Imagine your energies and their power to flow outward through the extension of your arms. What safety does that distance that separates you from the other provide? How does your sense of self change when your ability to act shifts to the edge of your extension from close to your core?

The art of Aikido speaks to relationships within the self and with the external. The core relates to the perimeter, the deep muscles with the superficial, the proximal joints with the distal. From the center of being, our influence extends through the power of the mind and the awareness it brings to our connections to distant realms. Our skills find expression at outward reaches that expand our sense of personal power. Relationships change as distance that measures our relative places expands or contracts, demanding, in turn, proportionate adjustments in timing. Angles and trajectories further expand the spectrum of expressive qualities. Within the realm of repetitive strikes and responses, *maai* colors our expression with nuance and complexity as we project or extend ourselves into our encounters. Contraction no longer shapes our response; extension expands our influence and power to direct. Extension nurtures a new self-image.

Extension has a push-pull power that unites the self and other. It leads us through movements as our eyes lead our bodies. In turn, extension shapes our encounters and provides the connection between my core and yours as my energy flows outward to align with your offerings. Docked with you, my extension takes up the slack and guides you through relinquished paths of exploration.

Extension shapes and nurtures a new self-image. Focus your awareness on the front surface of your body and extend it outward through your arms. Let the energy of your extension stay connected to your body so that both move connected to each other. Does that extension lead you into new ventures, into solid engagements?

Now shift your focus to the backside of your body. Extend out through your arms once again, but let your attention capture the behavior of the backside. Let it move forward in the same direction as the arms are extending, and feel the push of its involvement. Then let the backside have a diverging mind of its own. Let it lead as if it were the front side. Feel the contradiction in your movement as the backside no longer supports the forward extension through the arms. Now take the two options and incorporate their felt sense into an engagement. How do they each affect your blending, leading, and control? Hold on to those two felt experiences and choose one to enhance your self-image—and stay tuned in to the experience of the present moment.

———

Relax into your being. Whether sitting, lying, or standing, let your body sigh into a release of tensions. Relax to the support of the floor or the chair. Let go of your holds that impact your form—whether mental, emotional, or physical. Release from the armoring that controls your expression.

Breathe in and release. Let the breath fill you until the tension of expansion and holding succumbs to the demands of movement. And in that movement, withdraw to your core. Inhale again and feel the limits imposed by your patterns of holding. How far can you extend yourself? Is that limit the ultimate that your body can provide and your mind can conceive? Does my question entice you to doubt, freeing the mind to envision the unknown possibilities?

As you return from those limits to the security of home, feel for the path that the releases take. Do you effortlessly slide to your final sup-

port or do snags catch you, restraining you from some final contraction or smooth deliverance to your core? And in that rebound do you completely release to the supporting elements, or do shadows and illusions confuse and restrain?

Breathe in and out and listen to the story that your movement spins. Stay open, listen, question, and interpret until the story line describes and proclaims the experience that defines you.

And when the time feels right, move on to another experience. Inflate, absorbing breath and energy that have the power to expand to new reaches. See the emanations of the body's light push out against the constraints that hold you in. Widen the doorway that opens you to new felt experiences. Let the breath support the expansion, feeling when to expand and when to fill in. Be open to new grounding and extensions that organize new images of the self. Preserve those felt experiences and reflect upon them. Extensions shape our expression and alter our homes.

being present

I

What if something grabbed your attention? What would you do? Maybe you would stay tuned in to the experience, caught by its fascination, mesmerized by its spell, or pulled along by its action. So, let's let it happen and see where you go with your attention. There's no need to wait for any big dramatic event. Let your eyes fall upon the oak leaf that dangles from the limb by your window. Or maybe the sound of a passing plane will capture your ears, or a passing scent will waft beneath your nose. What happens next? Can you stay tuned in to the experience and see how it unfolds? Does it draw you in deeper into its mystery? Do you remain only an observer, intently focused with your eyes, or ears, or nose? Does the attention open you up to other sensations or observations that enlarge the experience? Or will impatience or foolishness release you to less demanding activity?

What if I grab you by the lapel or take your wrist within my two hands? What would you do? And if your plan failed, what else would you do? And if my stature and intent were to change—taller or shorter, heavier or lighter, stronger or weaker, evil or teasing, determined or nonchalant—what would you do?

"What ifs" can occupy our minds and challenge us just as newcomers will pepper Sensei with hypothetical situations. My Sensei refused to address "what ifs" or to acknowledge them as part of the training.

Life experiences are seldom, if ever, predictable in all their subtle or overt intricacies. As I wrap my two hands around your wrist, there can be many differences in my challenge. And each variation seeks its own identity in the response that it receives. Within a theme, true variations appear as we intimately experience the encounter with sensitive awareness. "What ifs" take us into the realm of the unpredictable future.

We cannot possibly anticipate and prepare for all possibilities; we can, however, prepare ourselves to deal with this which is at hand now. Training in the art places us in the present to deal with the situation as it presents itself in the immediate and intimate dialogue between you and other.

We develop more and more options for our responses as we mature in the art. Technique upon technique builds our catalog of responses and within each technique are variations in implementation. Within an engagement, which response do you choose? And which expression of that response is appropriate for the offering within the encounter? Choice cannot be made until the immediacy of the encounter evokes a counter that moves in synchrony with the energies of the challenge. Choice cannot be made until presence in the now fills out the lived moment.

But choice implies a judgment process where the value of options are weighed before action. How often do we choose our response before the attack unfolds; and how often are these choices found lacking in the full expression of mastery? Choices and options have learning value whereby "what ifs" become the exploration of form within our actions. In the moment of an encounter, however, there is no time to intellectualize, evaluate, collect your thoughts, gather your wits, or test a response. You are immersed in an unfolding reality and you have to deal with it. This is it *now*.

Practice is the process of establishing and assessing the value of options for action under different circumstances. It shapes our movement in response to various offerings. It develops interactive skills that free us from acquired conditioned responses. It takes a structured response and reveals within that structure the nuances that create unlimited freedom in our expression. The form of technique evolves into the freedom of continuous action—always present to and responsive to the now.

II

The John Lennon lyrics "Life is what happens to you while you're busy making other plans" brings home an important point. In the process of planning for the future, worrying about hitting the goal, or being too concerned about executing a technique, we lose sight of what is happening in the current moment. We move on, lost to the experience of the moment that is full of sensations and opportunities waiting for our presence and acknowledgment. Too often our focus is given to beginnings and endings while the in-betweens go unnoticed. How many moments in our lives have we lost because we failed to fully engage them?

———

Kneel on your left knee upon a cushioned surface. Reach for the ground with your right hand and place it down flat just to the left of your right

foot with the fingers pointing back to you. Tuck
your chin in to your chest as you lean forward to
begin a forward roll. Support yourself as neces-
sary with your left hand upon the ground.

As the wheel-like form of your body advances
forward, the head rolls to the ground and the
torso follows the moving line of the wheel's
rim—along the right arm, diagonally across the
back to the left buttock, and onto the left knee.
Momentum takes you down and around until
the finish resembles the start.

———

Just a few lines are needed to lead you through a forward roll. Beginners worry about the wheel collapsing while the more advanced rush through the exercise to experience and show off their mastery. What is
it that makes it so difficult for some? And what is it
that you experience when you start and end in the
same position?

———

In your imagination, please roll forward; when
done, describe the experience. What sensations,
observations, concerns, and feelings did you have
as you approached the activity and as you ended
it? Roll again and again, and after each roll,
pause to describe the experience again. Was it

easy to describe what occurred at the start and at the finish? Did you feel anxiety at first, and later relief? Or did you feel confidence and then satisfaction for a task well done? Did you see yourself genuflecting to the earth and wobbling to a reassumed starting position? Or did you see the darkness of an entry and the light of the exit? Would you need a few words, a few lines, or a few pages to write about your experience? Could you paint your observations, play back the sounds, or gauge your contacts with the ground?

And what about those moments between the start and the end? What can you say about them? Were you open to that experience or did you shut down your awareness once you threw yourself into the activity? Where were your eyes looking when you reached down and when the head rolled close to the ground and the buttocks saluted the sky? And what did you see? Did you follow the point-by-point contacts between body and ground as your wheel traveled its course? Did you feel the serenity of unrushed time travel or was time experienced in the rush of quantum leaps? Could you notice obstacles that came upon your path and could you alter the course of your travels?

———

Presence is that quality of being that arises from the awareness that we bring to our actions. It brings new meaning to the space between beginning and end, between birth and death.

III

Now begin to see yourself waiting there in a kneeling position on the mat. Still gasping for a breath, you try to settle yourself down. Your mouth is dry as if you hadn't touched water in days while your skin is profusely pouring out sweat. It's hot and the air is heavy.

At the opposite end of the mat, about twenty feet away, five other kneeling individuals are facing you. You know they are anxious to charge you, to pounce upon you, to challenge you to prove your worth. Along the left border of the mat there are perhaps two dozen observers seated haphazardly while over there, diagonally to your right front, sit the two judges—the head instructor and a visiting Sensei.

You've often thought about what would happen next during the period of training in anticipation of this test. You decided that your strategy would be somehow different in response to the expected charge. You thought that you could differentiate yourself and demonstrate your uniqueness and creativity. Perhaps you could execute your evasive and defensive techniques from a kneeling position for as long as possible. This is not working from your strength but it would give you some indication of your progress along the path of practice. Yes, that would be an interesting strategy—at least, up to the present moment. Are you ready to stay with it, or will you cave in to the moment and just move for survival?

You scan the horizon of waiting attackers. You didn't quite expect this collection of assailants. There are some there that would move easily and would not present too great a challenge. However, there are some others—well, you know you could expect quite the opposite. Daring and demanding, they will use their physical stature and their intent to test your mettle and skills.

You see them waiting there in restraints, waiting for your bow to release them and start the test. You wonder if you can wait them out and upset their balance. You want to rest a bit longer and get yourself more under control. But you feel the eyes of everyone upon you, waiting for you to get things started.

You yield to the perceived pressures of the audience and impatient attackers as you move your left hand from your knee to a spot on the floor in front of you. That movement in itself was enough to begin the process. You try to complete your bow in a composed manner, but you sense that the attackers are already rushing themselves through their bows and are already charging you. Before you can look up from your bow the action shatters your composure. Your preformed strategy disappears, lost in the history of thought and imagination. Survival demands movement as you thrust yourself into the oncoming surge.

The tall one on the left catches your attention first. Only a few steps are needed for him to close the distance. His attack, packaged with a gleam in his eye, begins as he raises his right arm to strike you on the head. . . .

The test continued within distortions of time. Waiting moments seemed exceedingly long and forced movement before its time. And action moments stretched to the limits of exhaustion as seconds lived on as minutes.

The action was fast as anxiety and self-protection sped you through one encounter after another. No time to experience the engagements, only to dispatch them. The rush of speed determined movement and clouded the experience of each encounter.

Your focus was pulled in different directions. The closing attack demanded your presence while the potentiality of others created distractions that affected the quality of your engagements. Balance between near and far, internal and external, local and general wanted to provide its support but got neglected for the squirrel-like movements of the mind.

How do we learn to stay with and within the experience?

————

Words, perceptions, and expectations color our experiences and give reality a meaning removed from the stillness of just being. Words describe the dry mouth, the hot and heavy air, and the gasping for a breath, creating a reality fortified by descriptors that ensure discomfort and displacement from inner tranquility.

Time leaps forward, taking us from the beginning to end through blind alleys that connect distant moments. Partnered with anxiety, it forces action toward goals or ends and creates gaps in our experience. The throw becomes the treasured goal of action rather than the natural evolution of a course of action to which we are forever present. Gaps arise between the beginning and the end, the start of a roll and the final slap against the floor, and between the onset of the attack and the final takedown. Gaps have content, information, and messages that we cannot heed. Gaps have a beauty that we do not see or an impact that we cannot assess. Movement progresses, but beyond control and equilibrium, in a precipitous and programmed manner.

Power returns as awareness lights up the dark alleys of encounters and engagements. Note the context within which energy flows as it waits for its final disposition. Observe as awareness illuminates those passages, changing giant leaps forward into manageable steps. Listen to the dialogue that fills in the encounter. Relax into the comfort that time is a measure but not reality and that in those smaller measures the magnitude of events diminish. Effort responds in like manner to the smaller demands of each lived moment.

Living in the moment requires a mental conditioning that being present provides. There is no need to compose yourself, to pause for another breath, or to get ready for another encounter. Being present removes the demands of getting ready and the trauma of the unexpected. It places the spirit within each living moment and always engages the events that happen. Being present establishes a new center from which self-expression emerges.

IV

Living in the moment removes the concerns for the past and the anxiety about the future. It establishes a presence to witness and engage what is before us at this moment. Action slows down to provide insights into the gaps of our existence. And in the slower pacing, we see more clearly the unfolding of events that impinge our reality. All that is external merges with an inner awareness, bringing greater understanding and wiser response to each engagement. Engage each energy, movement, and action with the clarity of new perceptions. Enter and blend with the confidence that the new timing presents.

As the encounter approaches, the inner clock of presence distorts the measured time to allow greater opportunities for response in a more relaxed manner. Options appear in shaping the response as the distant, end result no longer determines behavior. Unattached to the end or to the encounter, the practitioner stays ever-present to the shifts and turns of the interaction, always ready to react to the presented opportunities.

Now enjoy the experience of a backward roll or feast upon the sensations and dialogue of an imagined attack. Let the event occur within an altered time in which you experience the slow unfolding of movement that allows you to relax into its flow. Feel for the contacts between the self and the ground or between the self and other, and witness your confident response to the messages and opportunities that you receive. Take in the worlds that your watchful presence sees, and know that within the intimacy of this presence emerges the protection and expression of the true self. Within the realm of your imagination feel the growth of maturity in your art and wake up to its truth in the realms your presence engages.

self-defense
and a sense of self

I

*It didn't matter whether the path was smooth
and clear or rough and covered with brush. It
didn't matter whether the terrain was flat or
steep. It didn't matter if we were going through
the poorly defined edge where rough terrain
became a rocky brook bed. Molly embraced the
trail with unbridled vigor. I wanted for her to
slow down and to be careful, but her innate tendency was to move forward knowing that everything would be all right. Supported by such
trust, she enjoyed her romps. She appeared to
enjoy the freedom in her movement and her
interaction with the terrain. She seemed to*

know that she could always adjust to whatever she would encounter. Molly was Molly as only Molly could be. There was no leash on her. There were no marked trails that defined where she could run. There was no invisible leash that reeled her in whenever she started to stray. She had a trust in the universe and she was going to enjoy herself.

––––

What does your posture and movement reveal about yourself? How does it reflect your view of the world and the way by which you will interact with that world? What does your coat of arms, emblazoned within the form of your movement, say about the truth of your essence?

Our actions and movement speak of our self-defenses—those behaviors that ensure the preservation of the expressions that served us well as we created our own personal histories. Every practitioner of the art of Aikido has a personal way of moving and engaging that goes beyond differences in physical stature. The art is a path leading to awareness of these expressions and the gestures that protect a manifested self and to a discovery of the connection between the true essence and expressed self.

The practice of the art takes us on an inward journey, beyond the physical realm of the practice, to the center of our being from which all true expression arises. Through it we become aware of our movements and interactions and the feedback they provide about the issues that organize our expressions. Behind the mask by which we are known to ourselves and to the world lies a truth. This truth is full of potential for being, living, and acting and it lies constrained by past conditioning of self-preservation.

Through the practice of the art, self-expression gains greater maturity and freedom as the seed's encasement is discarded, allowing for the growth and expression of the essence within its core. Freed from protecting constraints, essence merges with and engages the flow of the universe.

Through the practice of the art we learn how to trust that we can engage life with a sense of survival and enjoyment. And through the practice of the art we find ways to defend and express the true essence of our being.

II

Where do we begin to tell our personal stories? Should we start at the end, or would it be better to start at the beginning? But perhaps the beginning and the end are really the same just as the start and finish of a roll place the practitioner in the same posture. It's what happens in the middle that provides the story, its plot, its conflicts, and its unresolved issues. The innocence of birth passes quickly as survival strategies develop to deal with the forces that vie for the right to shape us. Layer upon layer of self-protection builds our character and its expression. External forces organize our structure, values, thinking, and movement. And in the end, do we have the strength to retain the organization that we created to protect the self? Or do we release ourselves from these forces and revert to the simplicity at our conception? In like manner, our art develops as we build technique upon technique. Test requirements demand five techniques against each attack, but in the end the power of no technique captures our fancy.

We are accumulators. We acquire stuff and hold on to it for periods much longer than necessity demands. At times we may commit to a housecleaning and sort through the possessions in our attics, cellars, and garages to discard the less valuable and make room for new collections. Similarly, our bodies become the storage places of behaviors that served us well at some time. These patterns of actions come to define the self that was forged when the self engaged its environment. We hold on to these patterns, perhaps longer than necessary, as essence is eventually identified with these trappings. Our movement manifests this identity that we hold onto with all our available physical and emotional strength.

To clear away these holdings brings new freedom in our actions. We strive for such freedom as we look for greater expression of potential and essence. We struggle to achieve yet are blind to the realization that struggle requires more energy than freedom does. We tire of preserving what is fundamentally unnatural to our essence and summon all the available strength and energy to hold on to what we may have unwittingly acquired as natural patterns of organization and movement.

But the journey along the path of the art awakens a new sense of self and a new sense of engaging life. The path uncovers new freedom to act and a new responsiveness to living in the moment. And in this present moment we fully engage each encounter with the grace of an unburdened self.

It is hard to change our ways. Awareness brings new possibilities to light. Courage, commitment, and patience allow for the testing of new patterns of action. Yet without the dependence of dominating physical strength we must place our trust in some outlook or force that will guide us through each engagement. And we must act without fears, inhibitions, reservations, and uncertainties, without aggressiveness or competitiveness, and without inflated, deflated, protected, or fragile egos. These all require energetic support and will forever keep us from being who we truly are. They will keep us from trusting ourselves, being comfortable with ourselves, and being confident that we can engage the flow of known and unknown events with personal safety and integrity.

In the *Tao Te Ching*, Lao Tsu said, "In the pursuit of learning, every day something is acquired. In the pursuit of the Tao, every day something is dropped." Is it time for you to drop some of your holdings and seek a freer and truer way of acting?

———

Feel your arm grabbed within the encircling hands of the attacker. Feel the strength and direction of the engagement. Don't think, don't worry, and don't try to figure out how you will deal with the situation. Just be present to the interaction and notice your contribution to the confrontation. To what extent are you supporting the attack with your own patterns of action, with your own behaviors that weaken your position and reinforce the intent of the attack? Can you feel your arm stiffen—maybe to display

your strength or to maintain a safe distance?
And can you feel the counteraction to your pat-
tern of expression? Your strength is interrupt-
ing the flow of the interaction. In trying to pro-
tect the self, you are immobilizing the self.
Might that not be the intent of the attack? So
why are you supporting rather than resolving
the engagement?

——

Through the practice of the art of Aikido, we find a simpler way of being and of acting. We release our- selves to the flow and trust that our awareness, blend- ing, skills, and freedom will lead us successfully through yet another encounter. We release to the force of gravity and relax into our being, trusting that as we catch and align with the flow, a new harmony will be established. And in the mystery of that har- mony we trust that power will emerge in unimagin- able ways.

——

After class, two practitioners engaged in a
freestyle practice to polish skills, to increase
stamina, and to simply enjoy the experience of
the art. The pace started slowly and the move-
ments were measured and precise. Breaths were

organized in synchrony with and in support of movement. Physical and mental freshness controlled the flow of the action. Techniques were clear and easily identified.

As the practice stretched into the second five minutes, the pace was clearly accelerating—not by design but by the lures that insidiously draw us away from our centers. Attacks became less precise not just from more exhausting efforts but from a desire to sneak in an unexpected trajectory to catch the defender on her heels. To some it may have looked like sloppy technique while to others it seemed like unknown mysteries of the art.

"What did you do there? What technique was it? How did you do that?" questioned the attacker. She had experienced a response to her attack that didn't match up with known techniques in her registry of defensive actions.

"I don't know," came the reply. "I wasn't trying to do anything in particular. I just did something but I'm not sure what it was. Did I hurt you? Was my response awkward?"

"No. I'm okay but whatever you did felt very powerful—taking the attack away from me and catching me by surprise. You received and blended in a way that I didn't quite understand but you effectively neutralized my attack."

"Thanks for your feedback. I wasn't trying to do anything other than to blend with your attack and ride it to a final resolution. Your body talked in its attack and I simply responded intuitively."

———

As we establish a new awareness, engage in genuine dialogues, blend, receive and lead, open to new options, and live in the present moment, we move from working hard to support struggle to making use of flow for more natural movement. These new insights and skills lead to an undoing of all that we have created within ourselves that no longer serves our new sense of self. Our acting becomes more fluid and genuine. Power comes from releasing ourselves from self-crippling ways of acting and from an uninhibited engagement of the flow. Evolution has shown that sheer mass and size do not ensure survival and triumph. Similarly, we cannot rely upon strength, resistance, and physical presence for our survival and our sense of self. The power to act comes with our ability to adapt to the situation at hand as we release to the most fluid and organic ways of engaging and acting.

The practice of the art is a vehicle by which we come to our true center and to the wisdom of graceful existence. It is not the practice that makes us comfortable with confrontations, engagements, and attacks; it is the comfort that we experience from finding our centers and ourselves.

III

Awaken to the tensions in your movement. Let the practice of the art lead to an awareness of the tensions that shape your movement and to a heightened sense of your potential as you release the holds of those tensions. Come to accept the natural power you possess and use more intelligently the true strength of your being. Come to understand the motivation and demands of authority but continue to pursue the quest for truth of yourself and the truth in and of your engagements.

———

Lie on the floor and release yourself from the effort to support yourself in gravity. Penetrate to the center of your relaxed being and give in to the support of the floor below. Slow, small movements are all that are required to realize those constrictions that suppress authentic movement.

Bend the elbow of your dominant arm and bring your hand near your shoulder with the palm facing the ceiling. Slowly extend your arm, lifting your hand toward the ceiling. As the arm approaches full extension, let the hand float forward so that the fingers point to the ceiling. Now release the arm and let it float slowly to its starting position. Move slowly as you pay attention to the smoothness and fluidity of your movement. Repeat the movement a number of times, always being attentive to the gracefulness of the movement. But perhaps instead of grace you noticed quivering, shaking, or unsteady movement as if you were encountering ruts, bumps, or detours along the path of the movement.

Now compare the same movement with the other arm and note the symmetry or asymmetry in your organization for action. When you are finished, rest for a moment and then explore another small movement elsewhere in your body—perhaps the simple rolling of the foot left and right, bringing the big toe toward the floor along your centerline and then the little toe outwards to the floor. Select your own small experiments to explore your organization for movement in different parts of your body. What sense of self does this investigation reveal?

———

Tai Chi forms popularize the act of slow movement for health and martial purposes. The unhurried, deliberate movement demands attentiveness to grounding, balance, and an organization for the weight shifts that relate fullness to emptiness. With practice, imperceptible reorganization within the physical and energetic make-up release the practitioner from limiting habits. Rather than being listless and lethargic, the slow movements open to greater power as energy supports full expression rather than to holding patterns of action.

What is the significance of such self-freeing to the concept of ki in our practice and in our lives? Would ki not be the unbridled flow of energy through our beings that represents the authenticity of our true power? Released and reorganized we seek the wholeness of innocent birth.

IV

It's scary to hear of deaths from heart disease and cancer of practitioners along harmony's way. What's missing? What don't we understand? Harmony within is just as important as harmony with the world out there. We need to listen to all channels—local and global. All are important to the health of the soul. All are needed for the relationships that nurture the whole.

———

The class proceeds as partners exchange attack and defend. Each pairing has its story of engagement and response. Each partner brings a perception of the self and other that shapes the encounter. Repetition can lead to learning but it more frequently leads to the entrenchment of old ways of acting. Notice the failed attempt to execute the defensive technique and notice how the following repetitions partake in the learning process. Is the pattern of acting reproduced this time with a little more force or extra momentum? Is false trickery invoked to sneak through the technique? Or is speed summoned to drag the attacker along in the wake of the technique?

———

Where is the courage to give up perceptions of strength and weakness and to search for more fundamentally sound ways of acting? What can we give up to allow new perceptions to enter our personal realm? And will the environment of partner, instructor, and peers support a new way of learning for each practitioner of the art?

Perceptions drive our behaviors; yet perceptions can deceive us as to the truth of the moment. I lie on the floor, relaxed into its support and organized into an image of symmetry. Yet the image belies the true asymmetry of my organization while it supports what I know as comfortable. Do your perceptions, comfort, and familiarities support a false image of self and its way of acting? Do they repress an unknown self with all of its power to act?

The way of the art leads to a healing, a restoration of harmony, and a cultivation of the true self. Contracting ways of acting give way to extension and a greater flow of energy. Tensions resolve, removing with them the weight of each situation. Repression of the self transmutes into the expression of the real self. Tranquility and harmony within establish a new self-image that engages anew the energy of the universe. This is Aikido.

moving within the experience of flow

|

In your imagination assume the identity of a large rock or boulder. Bring all your sensations of being a rock to your awareness. Experience the qualities that you attribute to the rock. Imagine its size, density, shape, solidity, and texture. Become the rock and feel your strength and immovability. (What human personality characteristics would you feel appropriate to your image of the rock?) Now with a full appreciation of these qualities, begin to generate some movement. How much effort do you need to expend to initiate motion? How much help do you need to rock yourself into motion? And once movement has been started, how do you keep yourself going? Do you rely upon gravity or momentum to traverse your path? Notice the landscape through which you are moving and imagine how you deal with what lies in your path. Then you hit an obstruction that stops your movement, steals your momentum, and challenges the power of your strength. What do you do to regain the moving experience?

Rest for a moment and clear the image of the rock from your imagination.

Now assume the identity of a large pool of water. Once again begin to feel all the qualities that you would ascribe to such a creation. Do you feel its coolness, fluidity, and its desire to extend and spread through, over, and around all that it encounters? Feel the effort that's needed to begin movement as you transition to new shapes that adapt you to ineffective constraints and to oncoming engagements. See how your fluidity changes you from a standing pool to a streaming presence, and feel your presence spread as if to permeate all that you encounter. Experience the power to transform yourself and to bring change to whatever you encounter.

Whether rushing forward or relaxing in quiet pools, whether charging with unbridled power or captured in unexpected eddies, whether passing through open spaces or encountering obstructions to your presence, your essence is a neverending and nonjudgmental flow.

———

Life is movement, and just as physical and mental stiffness or rigidity can bring a quick end to a freestyle exercise, they can also stunt the development of all other relationships. Essential movement, devoid of judgments and serene in its action, washes away the sense of self-importance that hinders all effective engagements. Essential movement receives and accepts what it encounters without concerns about goodness and rightness. Essential movement is the unhindered motion of the self that engages each encounter with relaxation and equanimity. Essential movement engages the flow of life with its interacting forces and serendipitous events that can change the course of our personal evolution.

We can choose our experience—with no judgments attached. We can engage the flow or we can wait in our place until something moves us. Or we can choose any other experience.

Flow is a moving experience. It is the universal progression of events, encounters, and engagements that constitute the known and unknown of our existence. It is the randori or freestyle exercise of the art—ever ongoing and unpredictable in its offerings. We can blend with the flow and interplay with each encounter, or we can struggle to control and to protect until the force of the flow overcomes us. As with the stream, we can adapt and shapeshift as we receive and blend with each encounter. Transitions are continuous, small, and sequential as we embrace the path of being. Unforeseen encounters are met with the fluidity and receptivity from which arise unimaginable powers to act.

How does the unimaginable dictate your behaviors? Do the "what ifs" paralyze your movement and stifle your being? Do you wait for initial resistance before you change your actions or do you engage with harmonious movement? Do you look upon your acting as a goal achieved, a job completed, or a task reluctantly handled? Or, like the stream, is the essence of your living a constant, never-judging, unperturbed, grounded, and balanced flow?

The rational mind is secure in the known and protects the self by choosing self-protecting actions. It trusts not the unknown and avoids the risks of dealing with the unfamiliar, unexplored, and unperceived. It acts as if each encounter provides only one opportunity for an unequivocally correct response. Does it only serve the conditioned self while sacrificing the soul to the constraints of a self-protecting prison? Does it not know that it has options for engaging each encounter? Does it not know that awareness of being present brings transitions that are safe and creatively self-expressive?

Understand flow with a felt sense. Let the kinesthetic sense of the stream lead you through each encounter, with its uncertain appearance and unimaginable offerings. Do it in a nonjudgmental, fully composed, and trusting manner. And in so doing, see how your manifested self changes as you continue to cultivate the true expression of your being? Let your expression be fluid in its transitions, elegant in its presentation, controlled at all times, and aesthetic and artistic in its appreciation.

II

I bowed, and with that gesture I committed myself to unknown engagements. I was ready to receive the unimaginable, continuous stream of offerings from those who were to test my mastery of the art. There was no further time to reflect upon plans as the first strike from the left came seeking the side of my head. Others waited their turn from attackers to my front and to my right. A wall constrained me to my rear.

Options related to where I would go were more important to me than those related to what I would do. Position was more important than technique. Position gave me more chances for survival and continuing movement than a classically administered technique.

I entered to connect with the strike before it reached its full extension toward its target. My entering and touch redirected the trajectory from toward my head to one aimed skyward. In close to the attack I was now able to safely move to its outside, thus placing me the furthest away from all of the attackers. Technique was an obstacle to my immediate need. As I entered I pivoted on my lead foot, sweeping a wide arc that searched for the edge of the mat. I connected with the attacker with a touch sufficient to make him move with the sweep of my movement. The separation between the attackers and myself was now bridged by the presence of the initial assailant. He moved with me, stayed to my front at all times, and served as a shield between the others and myself.

There was no need to rush into any continuing action. I was safe in my position, watching for the next encounter to unfold. The attackers changed their positions, trying to find an opening to their target. It was easy to move my human shield since he didn't know what to expect and since his focus was also shifting to protect himself from any oncoming attacks. My focus was soft as I took in the unfolding events.

My movement was constant within a small area—just enough to keep my shield in the most protective position. I could feel the connection between my shield and myself as I extended outward to make the connection that united us as one. My touch was directed as much by the changing forces of the encounter as by my desire to shape that encounter. I would stay active to create the unfolding reality and not submit to passive acceptance of unwanted and externally charged energies.

Given time, though, my shield began to redirect his efforts to attacking from his held position. His refocused action demanded attention and a response that maintained the existing relative

*relationships of the engagement. I let his move-
ment evolve until a new point of control presented itself. I took the opportunity that he presented, now changing my interaction with him
and my relationship to the other assailants. In
those few moments that seemed liked minutes, I
felt my breath moving easily and continued to see
my place in the unfolding events out there.*

*The other assailants kept searching for open-
ings to reach me, jockeying for positions that
would give a clear path and playing off of one
another to distract my attention and weaken my
shield. As their aggressiveness threatened the
security of my position, I chose to take the initiative. I changed the controlling hold I had on my
shield and cast him in the midst of the grouped
attackers. In my follow-through I continued my
motion, attentive to the next opportunity for an
engagement. It came faster than I would have
liked and it came simultaneously from two directions. I entered to accept the closest offering and to
establish a synchronized movement with it. I was-
n't concerned with the rightness of my response; I
only felt that it was an appropriate one consider-
ing the circumstances of the moment. It didn't
matter what the next encounter would bring since
its nature was still unknown. Could I trust that*

the way in which I engage the moment could shape the next encounter in my favor? And what was at hand was not to be an end but only a passing encounter in the flow of the larger event.

The harmony of our movement generated a force that cast him into the second attacker under the guidance of my extension. As the other attackers were momentarily frozen by the event that just occurred, my attention caught an opportunity to take another initiative. I feigned a strike to one of the assailants, upsetting his balance and exposing a place to take control of him. Without any reflection I chose to throw him into the crowd, letting the resulting scatter dictate the direction of my movement.

Frustration had finally driven the attackers to relinquish all restraints and to attack with more vigor. One after another they threw themselves toward me. And one after another I sidestepped, or pivoted around, or stepped back— always keeping the action going, unconcerned about rules, techniques, or any preconceived strategies. I needed to be nimble and elusive to keep myself alive and to wait for opportunities to establish more control.

Their attacks eventually converged simultaneously upon me. Instinctively I wanted to be outside of the collapsing circle. I chose a space between two attackers and extended myself into a forward roll that took me outside of the circle. My new relationships gave me the time and safety to prepare for the next encounter; that's all that concerned me at the moment. My movement and freedom gave me the chance to continue to be creative in engaging the unfolding flow of events.

———

Which way will the flow take you? Do you need to know? If so, why? Do your plans for engaging always work, and how do you plan for the unknown?

"What ifs" are of limited value because the real thing is living in the moment. Only this moment can evoke the appropriate response. The truth of the moment is found only in the moment and not in some imaginary preconceived thought.

The practice, then, becomes an improvisational theater or contact improvisational dance. The practitioner is prepared to engage any encounter, but at the same time is not prepared with the only and the right response. The attackers and the environment, together with the perceptions, values, and psyche of the practitioner, create the encounter and define the situation with which the practitioner must deal. All participants of the encounter immerse themselves into the engagement, creating responses to each communication in a fluid fashion. Improvisational acting is the expression of human freedom.

Accepting the uniqueness of each encounter, we must simultaneously reflect and act to generate intuitive responses based upon accumulated knowledge, experience, and primal understanding. While in action, we create an interpretive response that is congruent with our values, awareness, and capabilities. Within the training hall, the youngest students provide the lessons in spontaneity. They are less likely to get stuck in trying to figure out what to do in an attack. They are less inclined to intellectualize about their encounters. They are, however, more apt to engage the flow and continue within the flow, creating some responses that capitalize on flow and adapting others from learned lessons of the past.

Options have been spoken of as the keys to greater courageous expression. Yet options still carry with them the association with techniques, alternatives, and rational thought processes. Within the flow, there are no pauses for reflection and decision-making. Within the flow, reflection and action occur simultaneously. They are synchronized to each other, allowing for the timely, controlled response to the truth of the moment. What happens in each such encounter happens because it was a natural flow, because it seemed right, and because it was an appropriate response to what was sensed. Encounters become creative as a result of the freedom for true, uninhibited self-expression.

awareness of
and from the center

|

The path of the art of Aikido has revealed insights that go beyond physical exercise and domination of encounters. Skills in technique develop to provide a greater sense of mastery in the art. Yet the art asks for more as it shows the practitioner ways to release from structure, attachments, physical strength, and tensions. It leads to the relearned freedom to act effectively and tranquilly with the forces that shape our encounters. All in all, it leads to an awareness of who we are ("Self-Defense and a Sense of Self"), how we fit ("Perceptions," "Awareness," "Receiving and Blending," and "Controlling and Leading"), and how we choose to act ("Options and Change") or how we intuitively act

("Moving within the Experience of Flow") to creatively express the true self.

The art seeks harmony as the separation between the self and other gives way to a unification in which responsive action replaces domineering endeavor. Responsive and responsible action further imply engagements in which provided support strives toward reconciliation and resolution. In the outcome both attacker and defender, self and other, or self and object are no longer victims of circumstances.

Art becomes the path to self-expression. It demonstrates how to engage life and the universe. It teaches how to stay open to the message and how to adapt to any situation. And with this freedom of adaptability, each encounter is more likely to become one of harmonious and creative engagement, survival, and enjoyment.

In our personal development we strive to acquire knowledge, skills, capabilities, and possessions. In so doing, we rely upon acquired things for survival and betterment. But perhaps the objective of personal cultivation should be an undoing of the manifested self, defrocking it of all that hides the unconditioned true being underneath. And in this greater simplicity we come to realize true power and joy.

The practice of an art, whether Aikido or some other, is a path of discovery whereby awareness brings us to the center of our true being. I follow the path of awakening with the anticipation that increasing mastery brings greater understanding of the self, acceptance of its truth, and more harmonious and joyful engagements of life's offerings.

II

Halfway through the class, the instructor stopped the practice and had the students return to their kneeling positions in lines at the end of the mat. You could see that something was really on his mind and that he was preparing to address the group. He paced around a bit trying to collect his thoughts before speaking. The students used the pause to catch their breaths and to get a momentary rest from the earlier, fast-paced activity. Sensei then stopped, turned to the students, and began to speak slowly.

"When we as seekers of mastery in our art have reached the limits of our available power and abilities, the use of strength and speed no longer leads to learning but to further entrenchment of old ways of acting. If we fail to trust that new ways of acting are possible in ways that we cannot currently perceive and if we cannot step back and allow for the patient exploration of

new ways, then our art will never develop to the highest level. We will gain a certain level of proficiency that is adequate in some circumstances and enough to give us a sense of accomplishment and a desire to continue. But is that all there is to our art, to the art to which you have committed yourself?

"It's hard for us to move to new levels of mastery. I have seen your development over some months or over years. Yes, there are changes. You learn new techniques and you move with more confidence and you add more speed to your activities. You get your heart rate up and you get some exercise and you dwell in the apparent mastery of your skills. You rely upon momentum and you feel satisfied that you are blending and moving in harmony with the attack. You come to know your practice partners—their ability to move with ease, their tendencies, their patterns of movement—and you move as a practiced pair moves on a dance floor. However, are you satisfied that you have real power that will work in any circumstance? Or is your power restricted to the patterned encounters that you engage when you work with a particular partner or if you work in a comfortable setting?

180

"How much have you not tapped into yet? Do you know? And if I said to you that you have accessed only 10 percent or 20 percent of your true power, what would you think and do? Would it change your practice at all? Would it change the way in which you try to learn your art? Would it change the way in which you look at yourself to see if you are restricting yourself from the true realization of your power to act?

"I watch you practice day in and day out. I ask you to go slowly to become aware of yourself, how you organize and use yourself, and how you extend to meet your attacker. You comply with the advice to move slowly—at least for the first four or five repetitions. But then what happens? You begin to increase the speed of your practice until awareness takes a back seat to macho expression and you work yourself to near exhaustion. What have you learned? Maybe a new technique that you may or may not remember and that you may or may not ever use again in practice or a test or a real-life con-frontation. But are you any closer to mastery of the self, mastery of your organization of mind and body for action, mastery of the power to engage the unknown?

"With mastery there is control, but control does not mean speed or strength. Control comes from the ability to organize and move efficiently— letting the power of that organization direct the action and not the flailing of arms, or momentum, or upper body strength. When you go fast you encourage the latter and completely neglect the former.

"I can tell by the expressions on your faces and by your general body language that what I am saying is falling on some deaf ears. Some of you are trying to understand the meaning of my words, but you are still puzzled. Some of you think you understand and are motivated to leap to new levels of mastery, but in your earnest desire to get there soon you will lose awareness of my words and I will see you acting in old, familiar ways.

"Today I placed some constraints on your movement to encourage you to move in new ways. I deliberately took away your familiar source of power to act by asking you to keep your feet fixed, more or less, in one place while you engaged an attack. With such constraints you could no longer rely upon your legs to move a stiff organization of your torso nor could you rely upon the displacement of your body to gen-

erate momentum in the technique. Instead you needed to find new sources of power within yourself to allow you to engage the attack in new ways. The constraints were introduced to help you find the power of your center: the hips, pelvis, and waist. I asked you to become aware of the twist in your body and to find ways to use that twist to help you execute the technique. I also asked you to meet the attack in an unconventional manner—across the body—to help you organize your body differently and to encourage it to move in different ways. In so doing, I wanted you to realize that you could find new powers to act in previously unimaginable ways.

"And what happened? You all started slowly because it was new and because you had to see if you could replicate the movement that I had shown you. Very quickly, however, the speed of the practice began to increase, as you became more comfortable with the movement. But, unfortunately, with that speed came sloppiness. The feet began to move. The twist was flattened or straightened. Continuity in the movement disappeared and your movements became linear, back and forth, stop and go. And at each stop, each interrupt in the flow, you resorted to relying

183

upon strength and momentum to get you through the next phase of the technique. Each interruption of the controlled, reversible movement demanded a new preparation for restarting movement. The legs became stiff, the twist truncated, and the movement from your center escaped to the peripheral reaches of your shoulders and arms. It didn't take you long to give up the exploration of the new suggestions for movement. You were too drawn to the attraction of speed and its false association with control and mastery. You wanted exercise and gratification rather than learning. You readily gave up the opportunity to find new sources of power and new ways of expressing yourself.

"But that is your decision—one that you made on your own or one that you made in silent agreement with your partner. Or perhaps you found it necessary to move at the same pace as other practitioners in other pairings. Or, even more, you may not have heard what I was saying, or you may not agree with what I was saying, or you simply refuse to consider my suggestions. You all have your explanations and reasons, which I can accept. I only ask that you try to understand why you chose to act as you have and determine if it is for

your greater mastery of your art and greater cultivation of the self."

He glanced up at the clock and continued. "I have taken up a good portion of your training period with all of this talking. For the next few moments, stay in seiza or take up some other comfortable sitting position and please reflect on what I have said. To master an art you need to spend some time reflecting on the self to understand the ways, and possibly the reasons, for your expression."

Sensei then closed the training session and exited from the mat.

glossary

Aikidoka—An Aikido practitioner.

Atemi—A defensive strike to create an opening or to upset the attacker's balance.

Bokken—A wooden practice sword.

Dojo—A training hall.

Hakama—A pleated, divided skirt worn over a martial art practice uniform.

Irimi—An entering movement.

Jo—A wooden staff that's about five feet long.

Ki—Life energy.

Kokyu dosa—An exercise to coordinate breath and extension.

Maai—The distance between two individuals.

Nage—The practitioner who is attacked and who applies an Aikido technique.

Randori—A practice with multiple attackers.

Seiza—A sitting posture in which the legs are folded, knees slightly apart, and the seat is resting on the heels.

Sensei—The teacher.

Shiho nage—A four-direction throw.

Tenkan—A turning movement to align oneself with the direction of the force or attack.

Uke—The practitioner who attacks and becomes the recipient of a technique.

Ukemi—The act of taking a controlled fall, roll, or somersault when being thrown.

suggested reading list

Bertherat, Therese, and Carol Bernstein. *The Body Has Its Reasons*. Rochester, Vt.: Healing Arts Press, 1989.

Buber, Martin. *I and Thou*. New York: Touchstone, 1996.

Cohen, Bonnie Bainbridge. *Sensing, Feeling, and Action*. Northampton, Mass.: Contact Editions, 1993.

David, Catherine. *The Beauty of Gesture*. Berkeley, Calif.: North Atlantic Books, 1996.

Feldenkrais, Moshe. *Awareness through Movement*. New York: HarperCollins, 1990.

———. *The Elusive Obvious*. Capitola, Calif.: Meta Publications, 1981.

————. *The Potent Self.* New York: Harper & Row Publishers, Inc., 1985.

Goldstein, Joseph. *The Experience of Insight.* Boston: Shambhala Publications, Inc., 1976.

Goldstein, Joseph and Jack Kornfield. *Seeking the Heart of Wisdom.* Boston: Shambhala Publications, Inc., 1987.

Hanna, Thomas. *The Body of Life.* Rochester, Vt.: Healing Arts Press, 1993.

————. *Somatics.* Reading, Mass.: Addison-Wesley Publishing Company, Inc., 1988.

Heckler, Richard Strozzi. *The Anatomy of Change.* Boston: Shambhala Publications, Inc., 1984.

Homma, Gaku. *Aikido for Life.* Berkeley, Calif.: North Atlantic Books, 1990.

Ming, Shi, and Siao Weijia. *Mind over Matter.* Translated by Thomas Cleary. Berkeley, Calif.: Frog, Ltd., 1994.

Olsen, Andrea. *Body Stories.* Barrytown, N.Y.: Station Hill Press, Inc., 1991.

Ralston, Peter. *Cheng Hsin T'ui Shou: The Art of Effortless Power.* Berkeley, Calif.: North Atlantic Books, 1991.

Richardson, Jerry, and Joel Margulis. *The Magic of Rapport.* N.p.: Harbor Publishing, 1981.

Speeth, Kathleen Riordan. *The Gurdjieff Work.* New York: Pocket Books, 1976.

Spencer, Robert L. *The Craft of the Warrior.* Berkeley,
    Calif.: Frog, Ltd., 1993.
Steinman, Louise. *The Knowing Body.* Boston:
    Shambhala Publications, Inc., 1986.
Stevens, John. *Abundant Peace.* Boston: Shambhala
    Publications, Inc., 1987.
———. *Aikido: The Way of Harmony.* Boston:
    Shambhala Publications, Inc., 1984.
Ueshiba, Kissomaru. *The Spirit of Aikido.* New York:
    Kodansha International Ltd., 1984.
Westbrook, Adele, and Oscar Ratti. *Aikido and the
    Dynamic Sphere.* Rutland, Vt.: Charles E. Tuttle
    Company, 1970.

index

☾ REACH FOR THE MOON

Llewellyn publishes hundreds of books on your favorite subjects! To get these exciting books, including the ones on the following pages, check your local bookstore or order them directly from Llewellyn.

Order by Phone
- Call toll-free within the U.S. and Canada, 1-800-THE MOON
- In Minnesota, call (651) 291-1970
- We accept VISA, MasterCard, and American Express

Order by Mail
- Send the full price of your order (MN residents add 7% sales tax) in U.S. funds, plus postage & handling to:

  Llewellyn Worldwide
  P.O. Box 64383, Dept. 0-7387-0060-6
  St. Paul, MN 55164–0383, U.S.A.

Postage & Handling
- **Standard** (U.S., Mexico, & Canada)

If your order is:

  $20.00 or under, add $5.00

  $20.01–$100.00, add $6.00

  Over $100, shipping is free

(Continental U.S. orders ship UPS. AK, HI, PR, & P.O. Boxes ship USPS 1st class. Mex. & Can. ship PMB.)

- **Second Day Air** (Continental U.S. only): $10.00 for one book + $1.00 per each additional book
- **Express** (AK, HI, & PR only) [Not available for P.O. Box delivery. For street address delivery only.]: $15.00 for one book + $1.00 per each additional book
- **International Surface Mail:** Add $1.00 per item
- **International Airmail:** Books—Add the retail price of each item; Non-book items—Add $5.00 per item

Please allow 4–6 weeks for delivery on all orders.
Postage and handling rates subject to change.

Discounts
We offer a 20% discount to group leaders or agents. You must order a minimum of 5 copies of the same book to get our special quantity price.

Free Catalog
Get a free copy of our color catalog, *New Worlds of Mind and Spirit*. Subscribe for just $10.00 in the United States and Canada ($30.00 overseas, airmail). Many bookstores carry *New Worlds*—ask for it!

Visit our website at www.llewellyn.com for more information.

Teachings of a Grand Master

A Dialogue on Martial Arts and Spirituality

RICHARD BEHRENS

He can pin a man to the floor without touching him. He can stand on one foot and hold off twenty-two power lifters and professional football players. Considered one of the foremost martial arts masters in the world, he counsels Wall Street moguls, world-class athletes, even military hand-to-hand combat instructors.

Now Richard Behrens reveals the esoteric principles behind Torishimaru Aiki Jutsu, the only martial art in the world that allows its practitioners to control an attacker's movements and weapons without the use of physical contact. What's more, he shows how anyone can apply these same principles to everyday life events.

The book follows a question-and-answer format and is divided into four sections. The first focuses on the Torishimaru Aiki Jutsu and its novice techniques and principles of control. The second discusses meditation and the nature of the mind. In section three, Behrens shares thirty-three deep spiritual insights, and in section four he explains how to apply the martial arts principles to life and the world of business.

1-56718-060-4
416 pp., 6 x 9 $17.95

Yoga

The Ultimate Spiritual Path

SWAMI RAJARSHI MUNI

Formerly *Awakening the Life Force*

Yoga: The Ultimate Spiritual Path is a groundbreaking work for serious seekers and scholars about spontaneous yoga—the yoga of liberation. Instead of discussing the physical exercises or meditations usually understood to be yoga in the West, this book focuses on a proven process by which you can achieve liberation from the limitations of time and space, unlimited divine powers, and an immortal, physically perfect divine body that is retained forever.

The sages who composed the ancient Indian scriptures achieved such a state—as have people of all religious traditions. How? Through the process of surrendering the body and mind to the spontaneous workings of the awakened life force: prana. Once prana is awakened, it works in its own amazing way to purify your physical and nonphysical body. Over time, all the bondage of karma is released, and you become fully liberated.

1-56718-441-3
224 pp., 7½ x 9⅛, illus. $14.95

To order, call 1-800-THE MOON
Prices subject to change without notice

Yoga for Athletes
Secrets of an Olympic Coach

ALADAR KOGLER, PH.D.

Whether you train for competition or participate in a sport for the pure pleasure of it, here is a holistic training approach that unifies body and mind through yoga for amazing results. The yoga exercises in this book not only provide a greater sense of well-being and deeper unity of body, mind, and spirit, they also increase your body's ability to rejuvenate itself for overall fitness. Use the yoga asanas for warm-up, cool-down, regeneration, compensation of muscle dysbalances, prevention of injuries, stimulation of internal organs, or for increasing your capacity for hard training. You will experience the remarkable benefits of yoga that come from knowing yourself and knowing that you have the ability to control your autonomic, unconscious functions as you raise your mental and physical performance to new heights. Yoga is also the most effective means for accomplishing the daily practice of concentration. Yoga training plans are outlined for twenty-seven different sports.

1-56718-387-5
336 pp., 6 x 9, photos $12.95